THE LIFE OF
ROBERT MURRAY M'CHEYNE

THE LIFE OF
ROBERT MURRAY M'CHEYNE

ANDREW A. BONAR

THE BANNER OF TRUTH TRUST

THE BANNER OF TRUTH TRUST
3 Murrayfield Road, Edinburgh EH12 6EL
PO Box 621, Carlisle, Pennsylvania 17013, U.S.A.

*

First published 1844
First Banner of Truth paperback edition 1960
Reprinted 1962
Reprinted 1972
Reprinted 1978
Reprinted 1990
ISBN 0 85151 085 X

*

Printed in Great Britain by
BPCC Hazell Books
Aylesbury, Bucks, England
Member of BPCC Ltd.

CONTENTS

CONTENTS

INTRODUCTION

WHEN, on 25th March 1843, Robert Murray M'Cheyne died at the age of twenty-nine, it was inevitable that men should turn to Andrew Bonar for a Memoir of the one whose brief ministry of seven-and-a-half years had "stamped an indelible impress on Scotland." Both men were born in Edinburgh, Bonar three years before M'Cheyne, and after an education at the High School and University they entered the Divinity Hall in the autumn of 1831. From that point onwards they were the closest friends. They met with a few others every Saturday morning at half-past six for Bible study, together they sought out the spiritually needy in the poor quarters of the city, and they exhorted one another to the pursuit of that personal holiness which was to be so characteristic of their future lives. Already it was their mutual conviction that "it is not great talents God blesses so much as great likeness to Jesus," and their common aim was to live near to Christ. At the end of their course, in 1835, their ways temporarily diverged; Bonar went southwards to aid the minister at Jedburgh and M'Cheyne westwards to assist in the parishes of Larbert and Dunipace near Stirling.

In the autumn of 1836 M'Cheyne was called to his historic pastorate of St. Peter's, Dundee, and immediately we find him inviting Bonar to make the first of many visits; "I subjoin a map that you may find the house where I live; it is about five minutes' walk further west than the church—the west-most lane in Dundee going down to the sea." Two years later M'Cheyne was offered a charge in the not far off beautiful village of Collace in Perthshire. He declined the invitation but secured it for his friend Andrew Bonar and thus once more they were settled within easy reach of each other. In 1839 they went together, with two other Church of Scotland ministers, to Palestine for six months, to explore the possibilities of missionary work. In their absence a revival commenced in Dundee and, not long after their return, in

3

some measure, at Collace. This brought the two pastors into even closer fellowship, and they often rode over to assist one another.[1] On one occasion as M'Cheyne arrived at the door of the Collace manse on a wintry day, he said, "I have been riding all the way to-day through the pure white snow, and that verse has been in my mind all the time, 'Wash me, and I shall be whiter than snow'". Years afterwards Andrew Bonar's old servant used to describe M'Cheyne's last visit to Collace. "He preached in the church on 'Lest I myself should be a castaway', and the folk were standin' out to the gate, and the windows were pulled down that those outside might hear. I had to come awa' after he began, and I could see from the house the kirk lichted up, and oh, I wearied sair for them to come hame! They stayed at the kirk that nicht till eleven. The folk couldna gi'e ower listenin', and Mr M'Cheyne couldna gi'e ower speakin'. I mind the time when Mr Bonar couldna get his tea ta'en for folk comin' and speerin'[2] if conversion was true. Oh, to hear Mr M'Cheyne at prayers in the mornin'! It was as if he could never gi'e ower, he had sae muckle to ask. Ye would hae thocht the very walls would speak again. He used to rise at six on the Sabbath mornin', and go to bed at twelve at night, for he said he likit to have the whole day alone with God."

Andrew Bonar outlived M'Cheyne by nearly fifty years. He laboured on in Collace till 1856, then amongst Glasgow's multitudes he worked with the same undiminished prayerfulness that had characterized his Perthshire ministry, until his death in 1892. But throughout the course of his long ministry the memory and example of the friend of his youth never left him. "Life has lost half its joys, were it not the hope of saving souls," he wrote on that sad March day in 1843. "There was no friend whom I loved like him." Nearly forty years later

[1] It is interesting to note that during the times of revival of this period Isabella Dickson, who became Andrew Bonar's wife in 1848, was converted. Recalling her first impression of M'Cheyne, she later told her husband, "There was something singularly attractive about Mr M'Cheyne's holiness. It was not his matter nor his manner either that struck me; it was just the *living epistle of Christ*—a picture so lovely, I felt I would have given all the world to be as he was, but knew all the time I was dead in sins."

[2] Asking.

4

when Bonar was visiting the scenes of Jonathan Edwards' ministry in America, we find such comments as these in his Diary: "Saturday, 20th August 1881—How deeply interested would Robert M'Cheyne have been today had he been with us! he who used to speak of this place. It was really strange to me and wonderful that this morning I should be on the way to Northampton where so much work was done for God in other days. The day was beautiful, everything bathed in sunshine . . . We came to what was the old street where Jonathan Edwards' house stood . . ." The next day his thoughts were still dwelling on old memories when he wrote: "Filled with alarm and regret in reviewing the Lord's mercies to me, in using me to write the *Memoir of R. M. M'Cheyne,* for which I am continually receiving thanks from ministers. Why was I commissioned to write that book? How poor have been my returns of thankfulness. Oh, when shall I attain to the same holy sweetness and unction, and when shall I reach the deep fellowship with God which he used to manifest?"

Andrew Bonar's biography of M'Cheyne was written at Collace between the months of September and December 1843, and it conveys the fragrance of his life in a way that no later writer could ever recapture. It is as though a breath of the revivals which were then refreshing Scotland still linger over these pages, and as the reader is led back into the atmosphere of those times he is made to feel that the prayers which were once offered for the original publication are still being abundantly answered from on high.

Being dead, M'Cheyne yet speaks and it may be doubted whether any Christian can seriously read these pages without having an example of the power of godliness stamped upon his conscience in a manner that will abide with him all his days. So close was M'Cheyne's life and ministry to eternal realities that even with the passing of years and generations the importance of the lessons he taught abides the same. There is no doubt that could we regather the long departed flock at St. Peter's and summon back their pastor from the New Jerusalem, the message they would receive would be exactly as it was:

5

"Oh! brethren, be wise. 'Why stand ye all the day idle?' In a little moment it will be all over. A little while and the day of grace will be over—preaching, praying will be done. A little while, and we shall stand before the great white throne—a little while, and the wicked shall not be; we shall see them going away into everlasting punishment. A little while, and the work of eternity shall be begun. We shall be like Him—we shall see Him day and night in His temple—we shall sing the new song, without sin and without weariness, for ever and ever."

The Publishers,
August 2, 1960.

CHAPTER I

HIS YOUTH, AND PREPARATION
FOR THE MINISTRY

"Many shall rejoice at his birth; for he shall be great in the sight of the Lord."—LUKE i. 14–15.

IN the midst of the restless activity of such a day as ours, it will be felt by ministers of Christ to be useful, in no common degree, to trace the steps of one who but lately left us, and who, during the last years of his short life, walked calmly in almost unbroken fellowship with the FATHER and the SON.

The date of his birth was May 21, 1813. About that time, as is now evident to us who can look back on the past, the Great Head had a purpose of blessing for the Church of Scotland. Eminent men of God appeared to plead the cause of Christ. The Cross was lifted up boldly in the midst of Church Courts which had long been ashamed of the Gospel of Christ. More spirituality and deeper seriousness began a few years onward to prevail among the youth of our Divinity Halls. In the midst of such events, whereby the Lord was secretly preparing a rich blessing for souls in all our borders, the subject of this Memoir was born. "Many were to rejoice at his birth;" for he was one of the blessings which were beginning to be dropped down upon Scotland, though none then knew that one was born whom hundreds would look up to as their spiritual father.

The place of his birth was Edinburgh, where his parents resided. He was the youngest child of the family, and was called ROBERT MURRAY, after the name of some of his kindred.

From his infancy his sweet and affectionate temper was remarked by all who knew him. His mind was quick in its attainments; he was easily taught the common lessons of youth, and some of his peculiar endowments began early to appear. At the age of four, while recovering from some illness, he selected as his recreation the study of the Greek alphabet, and was able to name all the letters, and write them in a rude way upon a slate. A year after, he made rapid progress in the English class, and at an early period became somewhat eminent among his school-fellows for his melodious voice and powers of recitation. There were at that time catechetical exercises held in the Tron Church, in the interval between sermons; and some friends remember the interest often excited in the hearers by his correct and sweet recitation of the Psalms and passages of Scripture. But as yet he knew not the Lord, he lived to himself, "having no hope, and without God in the world." Eph. ii. 12.

In October 1821, he entered the High School, where he continued his literary studies during the usual period of six years. He maintained a high place in his classes; and, in the Rector's Class, distinguished himself by eminence in geography and recitation. It was during the last year of his attendance at the High School that he first ventured on poetical composition, the subject being, "Greece, but living Greece no more." The lines are characterized chiefly by enthusiasm for liberty and Grecian heroism, for in these days his soul had never soared to a higher region. His companions speak of him as one who had even then peculiarities that drew attention :—of a light, tall form—full of elasticity and vigour—ambitious, yet noble in his dispositions, disdaining everything like meanness or deceit. Some would have been apt to regard him as exhibiting many traits of a Christian character; but his susceptible mind had not, at that time, a relish for any higher joy than the refined gaieties of society, and for such pleasures as the song and the dance could yield. He himself regarded these as days of ungodliness—days wherein he cherished a pure morality, but lived in heart a Pharisee. I have heard him say that there was a correctness and propriety in his demeanour at times of devotion, and in public worship, which some, who knew not his heart, were ready to put to the account of real feeling. And this experience of his own heart made him look with jealousy on the

8

mere outward signs of devotion, in dealing with souls. He had learnt in his own case how much a soul, unawakened to a sense of guilt, may have satisfaction in performing, from the proud consciousness of integrity towards man, and a sentimental devotedness of mind that chastens the feelings without changing the heart.

He had great delight in rural scenery. Most of his summer vacations used to be spent in Dumfriesshire, and his friends in the parish of Ruthwell and its vicinity retain a vivid remembrance of his youthful days. His poetic temperament led him to visit whatever scenes were fitted to stir the soul. At all periods of his life, also, he had a love of enterprise. During the summer months he occasionally made excursions with his brother, or some intimate friend, to visit the lakes and hills of our Highlands, cherishing thereby, unawares, a fondness for travel, that was most useful to him in after days. In one of these excursions, a somewhat romantic occurrence befell the travellers, such as we might rather have expected to meet with in the records of his Eastern journey. He and his friend had set out on foot to explore, at their leisure, Dunkeld and the highlands in its vicinity. They spent a day at Dunkeld, and about sunset set out again with the view of crossing the hills to Strathardle. A dense mist spread over the hills soon after they began to climb. They pressed on, but lost the track that might have guided them safely to the glen. They knew not how to direct their steps to any dwelling. Night came on, and they had no resource but to couch among the heath, with no other covering than the clothes they wore. They felt hungry and cold; and, awaking at midnight, the awful stillness of the lonely mountains spread a strange fear over them. But, drawing close together, they again lay down to rest, and slept soundly till the cry of some wild birds and the morning dawn aroused them.

Entering the Edinburgh University in November 1827, he gained some prize in all the various classes he attended. In private he studied the modern languages; and gymnastic exercises at that time gave him unbounded delight. He used his pencil with much success, and then it was that his hand

9

was prepared for sketching the scenes of the Holy Land. He had a very considerable knowledge of music, and himself sang correctly and beautifully. This, too, was a gift which was used to the glory of the Lord in after days—wonderfully enlivening his secret devotions, and enabling him to lead the song of praise in the congregation wherever occasion required. Poetry also was a never-failing recreation; and his taste in this department drew the attention of Professor Wilson, who adjudged him the prize in the Moral Philosophy class for a poem, "On the Covenanters."

In the winter of 1831, he commenced his studies in the Divinity Hall, under Dr Chalmers; and the study of Church History under Dr Welsh. It may be naturally asked, What led him to wish to preach salvation to his fellow-sinners? Could he say, like Robert Bruce, "*I was first called to my grace, before I obeyed my calling to the ministry*"? Few questions are more interesting than this; and our answer to it will open up some of the wonderful ways of Him "whose path is in the great waters, and whose footsteps are not known;" Psalm lxxvii. 19: for the same event that awakened his soul to a true sense of sin and misery, led him to the ministry.

During his attendance at the literary and philosophical classes he felt occasional impressions, none of them perhaps of much depth. There can be no doubt that he himself looked upon the death of his eldest brother, David, as the event which awoke him from the sleep of nature, and brought in the first beam of Divine light into his soul. By that providence the Lord was calling one soul to enjoy the treasures of grace, while he took the other into the possession of glory.

In this brother, who was his senior by eight or nine years, the light of Divine grace shone before men with rare and solemn loveliness. His classical attainments were very high; and, after the usual preliminary studies, he had been admitted Writer to the Signet. One distinguishing quality of his character was his sensitive truthfulness. In a moment would the shadow flit across his brow, if any incident were related wherein there was the slightest exaggeration; or even when nothing but truth was spoken, if only the deliverer seemed to take up a false or exaggerated view. He must not merely speak the whole truth himself, but he must have the hearer also to apprehend the whole truth. He spent much of his leisure hours in attending to the younger members of the family. Tender and affectionate, his grieved look when they vexed him by resisting his counsels had (it is said) something in it so persuasive that it never failed in the end to prevail on those with whom his words had not succeeded. His youngest brother, at a time when he lived according to the course of this world, was the subject of many of his fervent prayers. But a deep melancholy, in a great degree the effect of bodily ailments, settled down on David's soul. Many weary months did he spend in awful gloom, till the trouble of his soul wasted away his body; but the light broke in before his death; joy, from the face of a fully reconciled Father above, lighted up his face; and the peace of his last days was the sweet consolation left to his afflicted friends, when, 8th July 1831, he fell asleep in Jesus.

The death of this brother, with all its circumstances, was used by the Holy Spirit to produce a deep impression on Robert's soul. In many respects—even in the gifts of a poetic mind—there had been a congeniality between him and David. The vivacity of Robert's ever active and lively mind was the chief point of difference. This vivacity admirably fitted him for public life; it needed only to be chastened and solemnized, and the event that had now occurred wrought this effect. A few months before, the happy family circle had been broken up by the departure of the second brother for India, in the Bengal Medical Service; but when, in the course of the summer, David was removed from them for ever, there were impressions left such as could never be effaced, at least from the mind of Robert. Naturally of an intensely affectionate disposition, this stroke moved his whole soul. His quiet hours seem to have been often spent in thoughts of him who was now gone to glory. There are some lines remaining in which his poetic mind has most touchingly, and with uncommon vigour, painted him whom he had lost—lines all the more interesting, because the delineation of character and form which they contain, cannot fail to call up to those who knew him the image of the author himself. Sometime after his brother's death, he had tried to preserve the features of his well-remembered form, by attempting a portrait from memory; but throwing aside the pencil in despair, he took up the pen and poured out the fullness of his heart.

ON PAINTING THE MINIATURE LIKENESS OF ONE DEPARTED

Alas! not perfect yet—another touch,
And still another, and another still,
Till those dull lips breathe life, and yonder eye
Lose its lack-lustre hue, and be lit up
With the warm glance of living feeling. No—
It never can be! Ah, poor, powerless art!
Most vaunting, yet most impotent, thou seek'st
To trace the thousand thousand shades and lights
That glowed conspicuous on the blessed face
Of him thou fain wouldst imitate—to bind
Down to the fragile canvas the wild play
Of thought and mild affection, which were wont
To dwell in the serious eye, and play around
The placid mouth. Thou seek'st to give again
That which the burning soul, inhabiting
Its clay-built tenement, alone can give—
To leave on cold dead matter the impress
Of living mind—to bid a line, a shade,
Speak forth not words, but the soft intercourse
Which the immortal spirit, while on earth
It tabernacles, breathes from every pore—
Thoughts not converted into words, and hopes,
And fears, and hidden joys, and griefs, unborn
Into the world of sound, but beaming forth
In that expression which no words, or work
Of cunning artist, can express. In vain,
Alas! In vain!
                    Come hither, painter; come
Take up once more thine instruments—thy brush
And palette—if thy haughty art be, as thou say'st,
Omnipotent, and if thy hand can dare
To wield creative power. Renew thy toil,
And let my memory, vivified by love,
Which Death's cold separation has but warmed,
And rendered sacred, dictate to thy skill,
And guide thy pencil. From the jetty hair

12

Take off that gaudy lustre that but mocks
The true original; and let the dry,
Soft, gently-turning locks, appear instead.
What though to fashion's garish eye they seem
Untutored and ungainly—still to me,
Than folly's foppish head-gear, lovelier far
Are they, because bespeaking mental toil,
Labour assiduous, through the golden days
(Golden if so improved) of guileless youth,
Unwearied mining in the precious stores
Of classic lore—and better, nobler still,
In God's own holy writ. And scatter here
And there a thread of grey, to mark the grief
That prematurely checked the bounding flow
Of the warm current in his veins, and shed
An early twilight o'er so bright a dawn.
No wrinkle sits upon that brow!—and thus
It ever was. The angry strife and cares
Of avaricious miser did not leave
Their base memorial on so fair a page.
The eye-brows next draw closer down, and throw
A softening shade o'er the mild orbs below.
Let the full eye-lid, drooping, half conceal
The back-retiring eye; and point to earth
The long brown lashes that bespeak a soul
Like his who said, "I am not worthy, Lord!"
From underneath these lowly turning lids,
Let not shine forth the gaily sparkling light
Which dazzles oft and oft deceives—nor yet
The dull unmeaning lustre that can gaze
Alike on all the world. But paint an eye
In whose half-hidden, steady light I read
A truth-inquiring mind; a fancy, too,
That could array in sweet poetic garb
The truth he found; while on his artless harp
He touched the gentlest feelings, which the blaze
Of winter's hearth warms in the homely heart.
And oh! recall the look of faith sincere,
With which that eye would scrutinize the page
That tells us of offended God appeased
By awful sacrifice upon the cross
Of Calvary—that bids us leave a world
Immersed in darkness and in death, and seek
A better country. Ah! how oft that eye
Would turn on me, with pity's tenderest look,
And, only half-upbraiding, bid me flee
From the vain idols of my boyish heart!

It was about the same time, while still feeling the sadness
of this bereavement, that he wrote the fragment entitled:—

13

"THE RIGHTEOUS PERISHETH AND NO MAN LAYETH IT TO HEART"

A grave I know
Where earthly show
Is not—a mound
Whose gentle round
Sustains the load
Of a fresh sod.
Its shape is rude,
And weeds intrude
Their yellow flowers—
In gayer bowers
Unknown. The grass,
A tufted mass,
Is rank and strong—
Unsmoothed and long.
No rosebud there
Embalms the air;
No lily chaste
Adorns the waste,
Nor daisy's head
Bedecks the bed.
No myrtles wave
Above that grave;
Nor heather-bell
Is there to tell
Of gentle friend
Who sought to lend
A sweeter sleep
To him who deep
Beneath the ground
Repose has found.
No stone of woe
Is there to show
The name, or tell
How passing well
He loved his God,
And how he trod
The humble road
That leads through sorrow
To a bright morrow.
Unknown in life,
And far from strife,
He lived;—and though
The magic flow
Of genius played
Around his head,
And he could weave
"The song at eve,"
And touch the heart,
With gentlest art;

Or cares beguile,
And draw the smile
Of peace from those
Who wept their woes;—
Yet when the love
Of Christ above
To guilty men
Was shown him—then
He left the joys
Of worldly noise,
And humbly laid
His drooping head
Upon the cross;
And thought the loss
Of all that earth
Contained—of mirth,
Of loves, and fame,
And pleasures' name—
No sacrifice
To win the prize,
Which Christ secured,
When he endured,
For us the load—
The wrath of God!
With many a tear,
And many a fear,
With many a sigh
And heart-wrung cry
Of timid faith,
He sought the breath:
But which can give
The power to live—
Whose word alone
Can melt the stone,
Bid tumult cease,
And all be peace!
He sought not now
To wreath his brow
With laurel bough.
He sought no more
To gather store
Of earthly lore,
Nor vainly strove
To share the love
Of heaven above,
With aught below
That earth can show.
The smile forsook
His cheek—his look

14

Was cold and sad;
And even the glad
Return of morn,
When the ripe corn
Waves o'er the plains,
And simple swains
With joy prepare
The toil to share
Of harvest, brought
No lively thought
To him.
*   *   *   *
And spring adorns
The sunny morns
With opening flowers;
And beauty showers
O'er lawn and mead;
Its virgin head
The snow-drop steeps
In dew, and peeps
The crocus forth,
Nor dreads the north—
But even the spring
No smile can bring
To him, whose eye
Sought in the sky
For brighter scenes,
Where intervenes
No darkening cloud
Of sin to shroud
The gazer's view,
Thus sadly flew
The merry spring;
And gaily sing
The birds their loves
In summer groves.
But not for him

Their notes they trim.
His ear is cold—
His tale is told.
Above his grave
The grass may wave—
*   *   *   *
The crowd pass by
Without a sigh
Above the spot.
They knew him not—
They could not know;
And even though,
Why should they shed
Above the dead
Who slumbers here
A single tear?
I cannot weep,
Though in my sleep
I sometimes clasp,
With love's fond grasp
His gentle hand,
And see him stand
Beside my bed,
And lean his head
Upon my breast,
And bid me rest
Nor night nor day
Till I can say
That I have found
The holy ground
In which there lies
The Pearl of Price—
Till all the ties
The soul that bind,
And all the lies
The soul that blind
Be   *   *   *

Nothing could more fully prove the deep impression which the event made than these verses. But it was not a transient regret, nor was it the "sorrow of the world." He was in his eighteenth year when his brother died: and if this was not the year of his new birth, at least it was the year when the first streaks of dawn appeared in his soul. From that day forward his friends observed a change. His poetry was pervaded with serious thought, and all his pursuits began to be followed out in another spirit. He engaged in the labours of a Sabbath-school, and began to seek God to his soul, in the diligent reading of the Word, and attendance on a faithful ministry.

How important this period of his life appeared in his own view, may be gathered from his allusions to it in later days. A year after, he writes in his diary: "On this morning last year came the first overwhelming blow to my worldliness; how blessed to me, thou, O God, only knowest, who hast made it so." Every year he marked this day as one to be remembered, and occasionally its recollections seem to have come in like a flood. In a letter to a friend (8th July 1842), upon a matter entirely local, he concludes by a postscript— "This day eleven years ago, my holy brother David entered into his rest, aged 26." And on that same day, writing a note to one of his flock in Dundee (who had asked him to furnish a preface to a work printed 1740, "*Letters on Spiritual Subjects*"), he commends the book, and adds—"Pray for me, that I may be made holier and wiser—less like myself, and more like my heavenly Master; that I may not regard my life, if so be I may finish my course with joy. This day eleven years ago, I lost my loved and loving brother, and began to seek a Brother who cannot die."

It was to companions who could sympathize in his feelings, that he unbosomed himself. At that period it was not common for inquiring souls to carry their case to their pastor. A conventional reserve upon these subjects prevailed even among lively believers. It almost seemed as if they were ashamed of the Son of Man. This reserve appeared to him very sinful; and he felt it to be so great an evil, that, in after days, he was careful to encourage anxious souls to converse with him freely. The nature of his experience, however, we have some means of knowing. On one occasion, a few of us who had studied together were reviewing the Lord's dealings with our souls, and how he had brought us to himself, all very nearly at the same time, though without any special instrumentality. He stated that there was nothing sudden in his case, and that he was led to Christ through deep and ever-abiding, but not awful or distracting convictions. In this we see the Lord's sovereignty. In bringing a soul to the Saviour, the Holy Spirit invariably leads it to very deep consciousness of sin; but then he causes this consciousness of sin to be more distressing and intolerable to some than to others. But in one point does the experience of all believing sinners agree in this matter—viz. their soul presented to their view nothing but an abyss of sin, when the grace of God that bringeth salvation appeared.

The Holy Spirit carried on his work in the subject of this Memoir, by continuing to deepen in him the conviction of his ungodliness, and the pollution of his whole nature. And all his life long, he viewed his *original sin*, not as an excuse for his actual sins, but as an aggravation of them all. In this view he was of the mind of David, taught by the unerring Spirit of Truth. See Psalm li. 4, 5.

At first the light dawned slowly; so slowly, that, for a considerable time, he still relished an occasional plunge into scenes of gaiety. Even after entering the Divinity Hall, he could be persuaded to indulge in lighter pursuits, at least during the two first years of his attendance; but it was with growing alarm. When hurried away by such worldly joys, I find him writing thus:—"Sept. 14.—May there be few such records as this in my biography." Then, "Dec. 9.—A thorn in my side—much torment." As the unholiness of his pleasures became more apparent, he writes:—"March 10th, 1832—I hope never to play cards again." "March 25th—Never visit on a Sunday evening again." "April 10th—Absented myself from the dance; upbraidings ill to bear. But I must try to bear the cross." It seems to be in reference to the receding tide, which thus for a season repeatedly drew him back to the world, that on July 8th 1836, he records—"This morning five years ago, my dear brother David died, and my heart for the first time knew true bereavement. Truly it was all well. Let me be dumb, for thou didst it; and it was good for me that I was afflicted. I know not that any providence was ever more abused by man than that was by me: and yet, Lord, what mountains thou comest over! none was ever more blessed to me." To us who can look at the results, it appears probable that the Lord permitted him thus to try many broken cisterns, and to taste the wormwood of many earthly streams, in order that in after days, by the side of the

17

fountain of living waters, he might point to the world he had for ever left, and testify the surpassing preciousness of what he had now found.

Mr Alexander Somerville (afterwards minister of Anderston Church, Glasgow) was his familiar friend and companion in the gay scenes of his youth. And he, too, about this time, having been brought to taste the powers of the world to come, they united their efforts for each other's welfare. They met together for the study of the Bible, and used to exercise themselves in the Septuagint Greek and the Hebrew original. But oftener still they met for prayer and solemn converse; and carrying on all their studies in the same spirit, watched each other's steps in the narrow way.

He thought himself much profited, at this period, by investigating the subject of Election and the Free Grace of God. But it was the reading of *"The Sum of Saving Knowledge,"* generally appended to our Confession of Faith, that brought him to a clear understanding of the way of acceptance with God. Those who are acquainted with its admirable statements of truth, will see how well fitted it was to direct an inquiring soul. I find him some years afterwards recording:—"March 11th, 1834—Read in the *'Sum of Saving Knowledge,'* the work which I think first of all wrought a saving change in me. How gladly would I renew the reading of it, if that change might be carried on to perfection!" It will be observed that he never reckoned his soul saved, notwithstanding all his convictions and views of sin, until he really went into the Holiest of all on the warrant of the Redeemer's work; for assuredly a sinner is still under wrath, until he has actually availed himself of the way to the Father opened up by Jesus. All his knowledge of his sinfulness, and all his sad feeling of his own need and danger, cannot place him one step farther off from the lake of fire. It is "he that comes to Christ" that is saved.

Before this period, he had received a bias towards the ministry from his brother David, who used to speak of the ministry as the most blessed work on earth, and often expressed the greatest delight in the hope that his younger brother might one day become a minister of Christ. And

18

now, with altered views—with an eye that could gaze on heaven and hell, and a heart that felt the love of a reconciled God—he sought to become a herald of salvation.

He had begun to keep a register of his studies, and the manner in which his time slipped away, some months before his brother's death. For a considerable time this register contains almost nothing but the bare incidents of the diary, and on Sabbaths the texts of the sermons he had heard. There is one gleam of serious thought—but it is the only one—during that period. On occasion of Dr Andrew Thomson's funeral, he records the deep and universal grief that pervaded the town and then subjoins—"Pleasing to see so much public feeling excited on the decease of so worthy a man. How much are the times changed within these eighteen centuries, since the time when Joseph besought *the body* in secret, and when he and Nicodemus were the only ones found to bear the body to the tomb."

It is in the end of the year that evidences of a change appear. From that period and ever onward his dry register of every-day incidents is varied with such passages as the following :—

"November 12.—Reading H. Martyn's Memoirs. Would I could imitate him, giving up father, mother, country, house, health, life, all—for Christ. And yet, what hinders? Lord purify me, and give me strength to dedicate myself, my all, to thee!"

"December 4.—Reading Legh Richmond's Life. 'Pœnitentia profunda, non sine lacrymis. Nunquam me ipsum, tam vilem, tam inutilem, tam pauperim, et præcipue tam ingratum, adhuc vidi. Sint lacrymæ dedicationis meæ pignora!'" ["Deep penitence, not unmixed with tears. I never before saw myself so vile, so useless, so poor, and, above all, so ungrateful. May these tears be the pledges of my self-dedication."] There is frequently at this period a sentence in Latin occurring like the above in the midst of other matter, apparently with the view of giving freer expression to his feelings regarding himself.

"Dec. 9.—Heard a street-preacher : foreign voice. Seems really in earnest. He quoted the striking passage, 'The spirit

19

and the bride say, Come, *and let him that heareth say, Come.'* From this he seems to derive his authority. Let me learn from this man to be in earnest for the truth, and to despise the scoffing of the world."

Dec. 18.—After spending an evening too lightly, he writes —"My heart must break off from all these things. What right have I to steal and abuse my Master's time? 'Redeem it,' he is crying to me."

"Dec. 25.—My mind not yet calmly fixed on the Rock of Ages."

"January 12. 1832.—Cor non pacem habet. Quare? Peccatum apud fores manet." ["My heart has not peace. Why? Sin lieth at my door."]

"Jan. 25.—A lovely day. Eighty-four cases of cholera at Musselburgh. How it creeps nearer and nearer, like a snake. Who will be the first victim here? Let thine everlasting arms be around us, and we shall be safe."

"Jan. 29. Sabbath.—Afternoon heard Mr Bruce (then minister of the New North Church, Edinburgh), on Malachi i. 1–6. It constitutes the very gravamen of the charge against the unrenewed man, that he has affection for his earthly parent, and reverence for his earthly master; but none for God! Most noble discourse."

"February 2.—Not a trait worth remembering! And yet these four-and-twenty hours must be accounted for."

Feb. 5. Sabbath.—In the afternoon, having heard the late Mr Martin, of St George's,[1] he writes, on returning home— "O quam humilem, sed quam diligentissimum; quam dejectum, sed quam vigilem, quam die noctuque precantem, decet me esse quum tales viros aspicio. Juva, Pater, Fili, et Spiritus!" ["O how humble yet how diligent, how lowly yet how watchful, how prayerful night and day it becomes me to be, when I see such men. Help, Father, Son, and Spirit!"]

From this date he seems to have sat, along with his friend

---

[1] He says of him on another occasion, June 8, 1834—"A man greatly beloved, of whom the world was not worthy." "An apostolic man." His own calm deep holiness resembled in many respects Mr Martin's daily walk.

Mr Somerville, almost entirely under Mr Bruce's ministry. He took copious notes of his lectures and sermons, which still remain among his papers.

"Feb. 28.—Sober conversation. Fain would I turn to the most interesting of all subjects. Cowardly backwardness: 'For whosoever is ashamed of me and my words,' &c."

At this time, hearing, concerning a friend of the family, that she had said, "*that she was determined to keep by the world,*" he penned the following lines on her melancholy decision:—

She has chosen the world,
  And its paltry crowd,—
She has chosen the world,
  And an endless shroud!
She has chosen the world,
  With its misnamed pleasures:
She has chosen the world,
  Before heaven's own treasures.

She hath launched her boat
  On life's giddy sea,
And her all is afloat
  For eternity.
But Bethlehem's star
  Is not in her view;
And her aim is far
  From the harbour true.

When the storm descends
  From an angry sky,
Ah! where from the winds
  Shall the vessel fly?
When stars are concealed,
  And rudder gone,
And heaven is sealed
  To the wandering one!

The whirlpool opes
  For the gallant prize;
And, with all her hopes,
  To the deep she hies!
But who may tell
  Of the place of woe,
Where the wicked dwell—
  Where the worldlings go?

For the human heart
  Can ne'er conceive
What joys are the part
  Of them who believe;
Nor can justly think
  Of the cup of death
Which all must drink
  Who despise the faith.

Away, then—oh, fly
  From the joys of earth!
Her smile is a lie—
  There's a sting in her mirth.
Come, leave the dreams
  Of this transient night,
And bask in the beams
  Of an endless light.

"March 6.—Wild wind and rain all day long. Hebrew class—Psalms. New beauty in the original every time I read. Dr Welsh—lecture on Pliny's letter about the Christians of Bithynia. Professor Jameson on quartz. Dr Chalmers grappling with Hume's arguments. Evening.—Notes and little else. Mind and body dull." This is a specimen of his register of daily study.

March 20.—After a few sentences in Latin, concluding

with, "In meam animam veni, Domine Deus omnipotens," he writes, "Leaning on a staff of my own devising, it betrayed me, and broke under me. It was not thy staff. Resolving to be a god, thou shewedst me that I was but a man. But my own staff being broken, why may I not lay hold of thine?—Read part of the life of Jonathan Edwards. How feeble does my spark of Christianity appear beside such a sun! But even his was a borrowed light, and the same source is still open to enlighten me."

"April 8.—Have found much rest in him who bore all our burdens for us."

"April 26.—To-night I ventured to break the ice of unchristian silence. Why should not selfishness be buried beneath the Atlantic in matters so sacred?"

May 6.—Saturday evening.—This was the evening previous to the Communion, and in prospect of again declaring himself the Lord's, at his Table, he enters into a brief review of his state. He had partaken of the ordinance in May of the year before for the first time; but he was then living at ease, and saw not the solemn nature of the step he took. He now sits down and reviews the past:—

"What a mass of corruption have I been! How great a portion of my life have I spent wholly without God in the world; given up to sense and the perishing things around me. Naturally of a feeling and sentimental disposition, how much of my religion has been, and to this day is, tinged with these colours of earth! Restrained from open vice by educational views and the fear of man, how much ungodliness has reigned within me! How often has it broken through all restraints, and come out in the shape of lusts and anger, mad ambitions, and unhallowed words! Though my vice was always refined, yet how subtile and how awfully prevalent it was! How complete a test was the Sabbath—spent in weariness, as much of it as was given to God's service! How I polluted it by my hypocrisies, my self-conceits, my worldly thoughts, and worldly friends! How formally and unheedingly the Bible was read—how little was read—so little that even now I have not read it all! How unboundedly was the wild impulse of the heart obeyed! How much more was the creature loved than the Creator!——O great God, that didst suffer me to live whilst I so dishonoured thee, thou knowest the whole; and it was thy hand alone that could awaken me from the death in which I was, and was contented to be. Gladly would I have escaped from the Shepherd that sought me as I strayed; but he took me up in his arms and carried me back; and yet he took me not for any thing that was in me. I was no more fit for his service than the Australian, and no more worthy to be called and chosen. Yet, why should I doubt? not that God is unwilling, not that he is unable—of both I am assured. But, perhaps, my old sins are too fearful, and my unbelief too glaring? Nay; I come to Christ, not *although* I am a sinner, but just *because* I am a sinner, even the chief." He then adds, "And though sentiment and constitutional enthusiasm may have a great effect on me, still I believe that my soul is in sincerity desirous and earnest about having all its concerns at rest with God and Christ—that his kingdom occupies the most part of all my thoughts, and even of my long-polluted affections. Not unto me, not unto me, be the shadow of praise or of merit ascribed, but let all glory be given to thy most holy name! As surely as thou didst make the mouth with which I pray, so surely dost thou prompt every prayer of faith which I utter. Thou hast made me all that I am, and given me all that I have."

Next day, after communicating, he writes: "I well remember when I was an enemy, and especially abhorred this ordinance as binding me down; but if I be bound to Christ in heart, I shall not dread any bands that can draw me close to him." Evening.—"Much peace. Look back, my soul, and view the mind that belonged to thee but twelve months ago —my soul, thy place is in the dust!"

"May 19.—Thought with more comfort than usual of being a witness for Jesus in a foreign land."

"June 4.—Walking with A. Somerville by Craigleith. Conversing on missions. If I am to go to the heathen to speak of the unsearchable riches of Christ, this one thing must be given me, to be out of the reach of the baneful influence of esteem or contempt. If worldly motives go with me, I shall never convert a soul, and shall lose my own in the labour."

"June 22.—Variety of studies. Septuagint translation of Exodus, and Vulgate. Bought Edwards' works. Drawing— Truly there was nothing in me that should have induced him to choose me. I was but as the other brands upon whom the fire is already kindled, which shall burn for evermore! And as soon could the billet leap from the hearth and become a green tree, as my soul could have sprung to newness of life."

June 25.—In reference to the office of the holy ministry: "How apt are we to lose our hours in the vainest babblings, as do the world! How can this be with those chosen for the mighty office? fellow-workers with God? heralds of his Son? evangelists? men set apart to the work, chosen out of the chosen, as it were the very pick of the flocks, who are to shine as the stars for ever and ever? Alas, alas! my soul, where shalt thou appear? O Lord God, I am a little child! But thou wilt send an angel with a live coal from off the altar, and touch my unclean lips, and put a tongue within my dry mouth, so that I shall say with Isaiah, 'Here am I, send me.'" Then, after reading a little of Edwards' works, "O that heart and understanding may grow together, like brother and sister, leaning on one another."

"June 27.—Life of David Brainerd. Most wonderful man! What conflicts, what depressions, desertions, strength, advancement, victories, within thy torn bosom! I cannot express what I think when I think of thee. To-night, more set upon missionary enterprise than ever."

"June 28.—O for Brainerd's humility and sin-loathing dispositions!"

"June 30.—Much carelessness, sin, and sorrow. O wretched man that I am, who shall deliver me from this body of sin and death? Enter thou, my soul, into the rock, and hide thee in the dust for fear of the Lord and the glory of his majesty." And then he writes a few verses, of which the following are some stanzas:—

I will arise and seek my God,
And, bowed down beneath my load,
    Lay all my sins before him;
Then he will wash my soul from sin,
And put a new heart me within,
    And teach me to adore him.

O ye that fain would find the joy—
The only one that wants alloy—
    Which never is deceiving;
Come to the Well of Life with me,
And drink, as it is proffered, free,
    The gospel draught receiving.

I come to Christ, because I know
The very worst are called to go;
    And when in faith I find him,
I'll walk in him, and lean on him,
Because I cannot move a limb
    Until he say, "Unbind him."

"July 3.—This last bitter root of worldliness that has so often betrayed me has this night so grossly, that I cannot but regard it as God's chosen way to make me loathe and forsake it for ever. I would vow; but it is much more like a weakly worm to pray. Sit in the dust, O my soul!" I believe he was enabled to keep his resolution. Once only, in the end of this year, was he again led back to gaiety; but it was the last time.

"July 7.—Saturday.—After finishing my usual studies, tried to fast a little, with much prayer and earnest seeking of God's face, remembering what occurred this night last year." (Alluding to his brother's death.)

"July 22.—Had this evening a more complete understanding of that self-emptying and abasement with which it is necessary to come to Christ—a denying of self, trampling it under foot—a recognising of the complete righteousness and justice of God, that could do nothing else with us but condemn us utterly, and thrust us down to lowest hell,—a feeling that, even in hell, we *should* rejoice in his sovereignty, and say that all was rightly done."

"August 15.—Little done, and as little suffered. Awfully important question—Am I redeeming the time?"

25

"Aug. 18.—Heard of the death of James Somerville[1] by fever, induced by cholera. O God, thy ways and thoughts are not as ours! He had preached his first sermon. I saw him last on Friday, 27th July, at the College gate; shook hands; and little thought I was to see him no more on earth.

"September 2—Sabbath evening.—Reading. Too much engrossed, and too little devotional. Preparation for a fall. Warning. We may be too engrossed with the shell even of heavenly things."

"Sept. 9.—Oh for true, unfeigned humility! I know I have cause to be humble; and yet I do not know one half of that cause. I know I am proud; and yet I do not know the half of that pride."

"Sept. 30—Somewhat straitened by loose Sabbath observance. Best way is to be explicit and manly."

"November 1.—More abundant longings for the work of the ministry. O that Christ would but count me faithful, that a dispensation of the Gospel might be committed to me!" And then he adds, "Much peace. *Peaceful, because believing.*"

December 2.—Hitherto he used to spend much of the Sabbath evening in extending his notes of Mr Bruce's sermons; but now, "Determined to be brief with these for the sake of a more practical, meditative, resting, sabbatical evening."

"Dec. 11—Mind quite unfitted for devotion. Prayerless prayer."

"Dec. 31.—God has in this past year introduced me to the preparation of the ministry—I bless him for that. He has helped me to give up much of my shame to name his name, and be on his side, especially before particular friends—I bless him for that. He has taken conclusively away friends that might have been a snare—must have been a stumbling-block—I bless him for that. He has introduced me to one Christian friend, and sealed more and more my amity with another—I bless him for that."

January 27. 1833.—On this day it had been the custom

[1] Son of the minister of Drumelzier—very promising and very amiable.

of his brother David to write a "Carmen Natale" on their father's birth-day. Robert took up the domestic song this year; and, in doing so, makes some beautiful and tender allusions.

> "Ah! where is the harp that was strung to thy praise,
> So oft and so sweetly in happier days?
> When the tears that we shed were the tears of our joy,
> And the pleasures of home were unmixed with alloy?
> The harp is now mute—its last breathings are spoken—
> And the cord, though 'twas threefold, is now, alas, broken!
> Yet why should we murmur, short-sighted and vain,
> Since death to that loved one was undying gain.
> Ah, fools! shall we grieve that he left this poor scene,
> To dwell in the realms that are ever serene?
> Though he sparkled the gem in our circle of love,
> He is even more prized in the circles above.
> And though sweetly he sung of his father on earth,
> When this day would inspire him with tenderest mirth,
> Yet a holier tone to his harp is now given,
> *As he sings to his unborn Father in heaven.*"

February 3.—Writing to a medical friend of his brother William's, he says—"I remember long ago a remark you once made to William, which has somehow or other stuck in my head, viz., that medical men ought to make a distinct study of the Bible, purely for the sake of administering conviction and consolation to their patients. I think you also said that you had actually begun with that view. Such a determination, though formed in youth, is one which I trust riper years will not make you blush to own."

"Feb. 11.—Somewhat overcome. Let me see: there is a creeping defect here. Humble, purpose-like reading of the Word omitted. What plant can be unwatered, and not wither?"

"Feb. 16—Walk to Corstorphine Hill. Exquisite clear view—blue water, and brown fields, and green firs. Many thoughts on the follies of my youth. How many, O Lord, may they be? Summed up in one—ungodliness!"

"Feb. 21.—Am I as willing as ever to preach to the lost heathen?"

"March 8.—Biblical criticism. This must not supersede heart-work. How apt it is!"

"March 12.—O for activity, activity, activity!"

"March 29.—Today my second session (at the Divinity Hall) ends. I am now in the middle of my career. God hold me on with a steady pace!"

"March 31.—The bull tosses in the net! How should the Christian imitate the anxieties of the worldling?"

April 17.—He heard of the death of one whom many friends had esteemed much and lamented deeply. This led him to touch the strings of his harp again, in a measure somewhat irregular, yet sad and sweet.

"WE ALL DO FADE AS A LEAF"

SHE LIVED—

So dying-like and frail,
That every bitter gale
Of winter seemed to blow
Only to lay her low!
She lived to show how He,
Who stills the stormy sea,
Can overrule the winter's power,
And keep alive the tiniest flower—
Can bear the young lamb in his arms,
And shelter it from death's alarms.

SHE DIED—

When spring, with brightest flowers,
Was fresh'ning all the bowers.
The linnet sung her choicest lay,
When her sweet voice was hushed for aye!
The snowdrop rose above the ground
When she beneath her pillow found,
Both cold, and white and fair—
She, fairest of the fair,
She died to teach us all
The loveliest must fall.
A curse is written on the brow
Of beauty:—and the lover's vow
Cannot retain the flitting breath,
Nor save from all-devouring death.

SHE LIVES—

The spirit left the earth;
And He who gave her birth
Has called her to his dread abode,
To meet her Saviour and her God.
She lives, to tell how blest
Is the everlasting rest
Of those who, in the Lamb's blood laved,
Are chosen, sanctified, and saved!
How fearful is their doom
Who drop into the tomb
Without a covert from the ire
Of him who is consuming fire.

28

                    The grave shall yield his prize,
                    When, from the rending skies,
                        Christ shall with shouting angels come
                        To wake the slumberers of the tomb,
                    And many more shall rise
                    Before our longing eyes.
                        Oh! may we all together meet,
                        Embracing the Redeemer's feet!

"May 20.—General Assembly. The motion regarding Chapels of Ease lost, by 106 to 103. Every shock of the ram is heavier and stronger, till all shall give way."

"June 4.—Evening almost lost. Music will not sanctify, though it make feminine the heart."

"June 22.—Omissions make way for commissions. Could I but take effective warning! A world's wealth would not make up for that saying, 'If any man sin, we have an advocate with the Father.' But how shall we that are dead to sin live any longer therein?"

"June 30.—Self-examination. Why is a missionary life so often an object of my thoughts. Is it simply for the love I bear to souls? Then, why do I not show it more where I am? Souls are as precious here as in Burmah. Does the romance of the business not weigh anything with me?—the interest and esteem I would carry with me?—the nice journals and letters I should write and receive? Why would I so much rather go to the East than to the West Indies? Am I wholly deceiving my own heart? and have I not a spark of true missionary zeal? Lord, give me to understand and imitate the spirit of those unearthly words of thy dear Son, 'It is enough for the disciple that he be as his Master, and the servant as his Lord.' 'He that loveth father or mother more than me, is not worthy of me.' *Gloria in excelsis Deo!*"

"August 13.—Clear conviction of sin is the only true origin of dependence on another's righteousness, and, therefore, (strange to say!) of the Christian's peace of mind and cheerfulness."

"September 8.—Reading Adam's *Private Thoughts*. O for his heart-searching humility! Ah me! on what mountains of pride must I be wandering, when all I do is tinctured with the very sins this man so deplores; yet where are my wailings, where my tears, over my love of praise?"

"November 14.—Composition—a pleasant kind of labour. I fear the love of applause, or effect, goes a great way. May God keep me from preaching myself, instead of Christ crucified."

"January 15. 1834.—Heard of the death of J. S., off the Cape of Good Hope. O God! how thou breakest into families! Must not the disease be dangerous, when a tender-hearted surgeon cuts deep into the flesh? How much more when God is the operator, 'who afflicteth not *from his heart*, [מִלִּבּוֹ], nor grieveth the children of men.' Lam. iii. 33."

"February 23—Sabbath.—Rose early to seek God, and found him whom my soul loveth. Who would not rise early to meet such company? The rains are over and gone. They that sow in tears shall reap in joy."

Feb. 24.—He writes a letter to one who, he feared, was only sentimental, and not really under a sense of sin. "Is it possible, think you, for a person to be conceited of his miseries? May there not be a deep leaven of pride in telling how desolate and how unfeeling we are?—in brooding over our unearthly pains?—in our being excluded from the unsympathetic world?—in our being the invalids of Christ's hospital?" He had himself been taught by the Spirit that it is more humbling for us to *take what grace offers*, than to bewail our wants and worthlessness.

Two days after, he records, with thankful astonishment, that for the first time in his life he had been blest to awaken a soul. All who find Christ for themselves are impelled, by the holy necessity of constraining love, to seek the salvation of others. Andrew findeth his brother Peter, and Philip findeth his friend Nathaniel. So was it in the case before us. He no sooner knew Christ's righteousness as his own covering, than he longed to see others clothed in the same spotless robe. And it is peculiarly interesting to read the feelings of one who was yet to be blest in plucking so many brands from the fire, when for the first time he saw the Lord graciously employing him in this more than angelic work.

We have his own testimony:—"Feb. 26. After sermon. The precious tidings that a soul has been melted down by the grace of the Saviour. How blessed an answer to prayer, if it be really so! 'Can these dry bones live? Lord, thou knowest.' What a blessed thing it is to see the first grievings of the awakened spirit, when it cries, 'I cannot see myself a sinner; I cannot pray, for my vile heart wanders.' It has refreshed me more than a thousand sermons. I know not how to thank and admire God sufficiently for this incipient work. Lord, perfect that which thou hast begun!" A few days after—"Lord, I thank thee that thou hast shown me this marvellous working, though I was but an adoring spectator, rather than an instrument."

It is scarcely less interesting, in the case of one so gifted for the work of visiting the careless, and so singularly skilled in ministering the Word by the bedside of the dying, to find a record of the occasion when the Lord led him forth to take his first survey of this field of labour. There existed at that time, among some of the students attending the Divinity Hall, a society, the sole object of which was to stir up each other to set apart an hour or two every week for visiting the careless and needy in the most neglected portions of the town. Our rule was, not to subtract anything from our times of study, but to devote to this work an occasional hour in the intervals between different classes, or an hour that might otherwise have been given to recreation. All of us felt the work to be trying to the flesh at the outset; but none ever repented of persevering in it. One Saturday forenoon, at the close of the usual prayer-meeting, which met in Dr Chalmers' vestry, we went up together to a district in the Castle Hill. It was Robert's first near view of the heathenism of his native city, and the effect was enduring.

"March 3.—Accompanied A. B. in one of his rounds through some of the most miserable habitations I ever beheld. Such scenes I never before dreamed of. Ah, why am I such a stranger to the poor in my native town? I have passed their doors thousands of times; I have admired the huge black piles of buildings, with their lofty chimneys breaking the sun's rays—why have I never ventured within? How

31

dwelleth the love of God in me? How cordial is the welcome even of the poorest and most loathsome to the voice of Christian sympathy! What imbedded masses of human beings are huddled together, unvisited by friend or minister! 'No man careth for our souls,' is written over every forehead. Awake, my soul! Why should I give hours and days any longer to the vain world, when there is such a world of misery at my very door? Lord, put thine own strength in me; confirm every good resolution; forgive my past long life of uselessness and folly."

He forthwith became one of the Society's most steady members, cultivating a district in the Canongate, teaching a Sabbath-school, and distributing the Monthly Visitor, along with Mr Somerville. His experience there was fitted to give him insight into the sinner's depravity in all its forms. His first visit in his district is thus noticed—"March 24. Visited two families with tolerable success. God grant a blessing may go with us! Began in fear and weakness and in much trembling. May the power be of God." Soon after, he narrates the following scene:—"Entered the house of ——. Heard her swearing as I came up the stair. Found her storming at three little grandchildren, whom her daughter had left with her. She is a seared, hard-hearted wretch. Read Ezekiel xxxiii. Interrupted by the entrance of her second daughter, furiously demanding her marriage lines. Became more discreet. Promised to come back—never came. Her father-in-law entered, a hideous spectacle of an aged drunkard, demanding money. Left the house with warnings." Another case he particularly mentions of a sick woman, who, though careless before, suddenly seemed to float into a sea of joy, without being able to give any scriptural account of the change. She continued, I believe, to her death in this state; but he feared it was a subtle delusion of Satan as an angel of light. One soul, however, was, to all appearance, brought truly to the Rock of Ages, during his and his friend's prayerful visitations. These were first-fruits.

He continues his diary, though often considerable intervals occur in the register of his spiritual state.

"May 9.—How kindly has God thwarted me in every instance where I sought to enslave myself. I will learn at least to glory in disappointments."

"May 10.—At the Communion. Felt less use for the minister than ever. Let the Master of the Feast alone speak to my heart." He felt at such times, as many of the Lord's people have always done, that it is not the addresses of the ministers in serving the table, but *the Supper itself,* that ought to "satiate their souls with fatness."

May 21.—It is affecting to us to read the following entry: —"This day I attained my twenty-first year. O how long and how worthlessly I have lived, Thou only knowest! *Neff* died in his thirty-first year; when shall I?"[1]

May 29.—He this day wrote very faithfully, yet very kindly, to one who seemed to him not a believer, and who, nevertheless, appropriated to herself the *promises* of God. "If you are wholly unassured of your being a believer, is it not a contradiction in terms to say that you are sure the believers' promises belong to you? Are you *an assured believer?* If so, rejoice in your heirship; and yet rejoice with trembling; for that is the very character of God's heirs. But are you *unassured*—nay, *wholly unassured?* then what mad presumption to say to your soul, that these promises, being in the Bible, must belong indiscriminately to all? It is too gross a contradiction for you to compass, except in word." He then shows that *Christ's free offer* must be accepted by the sinner, and so the *promises* become his. "The sinner complies with the call or offer, 'Come unto me'; and thereafter, but not before, can claim the annexed *promise* as his—'I will give thee rest.'"

"August 14.—Partial fast, and seeking God's face by prayer. This day thirty years, my late dear brother was born. O for more love, and then will come more peace." That same evening he wrote the hymn, *The Barren Fig-tree.*

[1] It is worthy of notice how often the Lord has done much work by a few years of holy labour. In our Church, G. Gillespie and J. Durham died at thirty-six; Hugh Binning at twenty-six; Andrew Gray when scarcely at twenty-two. Of our witnesses, Patrick Hamilton was cut off at twenty-four, and Hugh M'Kail at twenty-six. In other churches we might mention many, such as John Janeway at twenty-three, David Brainerd at thirty, and Henry Martyn at thirty-two. Theirs was a short life, filled up with usefulness, and crowned with glory. O to be as they!

33

"October 17.—Private meditation exchanged for conversation. Here is the root of the evil—forsake God, and he forsakes us."

Some evening this month he had been reading Baxter's *Call to the Unconverted*. Deeply impressed with the affectionate and awfully solemn urgency of the man of God, he wrote,—

> "Though Baxter's lips have long in silence hung,
> And death long hush'd that sinner-wakening tongue;
> Yet still, though dead, he speaks aloud to all,
> And from the grave still issues forth his 'Call.'
> Like some loud angel-voice from Zion Hill,
> The mighty echo rolls and rumbles still.
> O grant that we, when sleeping in the dust,
> May thus speak forth the wisdom of the just."

Mr M'Cheyne was peculiarly subject to attacks of fever, and by one of these was he laid down on a sick bed on November 15th. However, this attack was of short duration. On the 21st he writes—"Bless the Lord, O my soul, and forget not all his benefits. Learned more and more of the value of *Jehovah Tzidkenu.*" He had, three days before, written his well-known hymn, "*I once was a stranger,*" &c., entitled "Jehovah Tzidkenu, the Watchword of the Reformers." It was the fruit of a slight illness which had tried his soul, by setting it more immediately in view of the judgment-seat of Christ; and the hymn which he so sweetly sung reveals the sure and solid confidence of his soul. In reference to that same illness, he seems to have penned the following lines, November 24th :—

> He tenderly binds up the broken in heart,
> The soul bowed down he will raise;
> For mourning the ointment of joy will impart,
> For heaviness, garments of praise.
>
> Ah, come, then, and sing to the praise of our God,
> Who giveth and taketh away;
> Who first by his kindness, and then by his rod,
> Would teach us, poor sinners, to pray.
>
> For in the assembly of Jesus' first-born,
> Who anthems of gratitude raise;
> Each heart has by great tribulation been torn,
> Each voice turned from wailing to praise.

"November 9.—Heard of Edward Irving's death. I look back upon him with awe, as on the saints and martyrs of old. A holy man in spite of all his delusions and errors. He is now with his God and Saviour, whom he wronged so much, yet, I am persuaded, loved so sincerely. How should we lean for wisdom, not on ourselves, but on the God of all grace!"

"Nov. 21.—If nothing else will do to sever me from my sins, Lord send me such sore and trying calamities as shall awake me from earthly slumbers. It must always be best to be alive to thee, whatever be the quickening instrument. I tremble as I write, for oh! on every hand do I see too likely occasions for sore afflictions."

"February 15. 1835.—Tomorrow I undergo my trials before the Presbytery. May God give me courage in the hour of need. What should I fear? If God see meet to put me into the ministry, who shall keep me back? If I be not meet, why should I be thrust forward? To thy service I desire to dedicate myself over and over again."

"March 1.—Bodily service. What change is there in the heart! Wild, earthly affections there are here; strong, coarse passions; bands both of iron and silk. But I thank thee, O my God, that they make me cry, 'O wretched man!' Bodily weakness, too, depresses me."

"March 29.—College finished on Friday last. My last appearance there. Life itself is vanishing fast. Make haste for eternity."

In such records as these, we read God's dealings with his soul up to the time when he was licensed to preach the gospel. His preparatory discipline, both of heart and of intellect, had been directed by the Great Head of the Church in a way that remarkably qualified him for the work he was to perform in the vineyard.

His soul was prepared for the awful work of the ministry by much prayer, and much study of the Word of God; by affliction in his person; by inward trials and sore temptations; by experience of the depth of corruption in his own heart; and by discoveries of the Saviour's fullness of grace. He learnt experimentally to ask—"Who is he that overcometh the world, but he that believeth that Jesus is the Son of God." 1 John v. 5. During the four years that followed his awakening, he was oftentimes under the many waters, but was ever raised again by the same Divine hand that had drawn him out at the first, till at length, though still often violently tossed, the vessel was able steadily to keep the summit of the wave. It appears that he learnt the way of salvation experimentally, ere he knew it accurately by theory and system ; and thus no doubt it was that his whole ministry was little else than a giving out of his own inward life.

The Visiting Society noticed above was much blessed to the culture of his soul, and not less so the Missionary Association and the Prayer Meeting connected with it. None were more regular at the hour of prayer than he, and none more frequently led up our praises to the throne. He was for some time Secretary to the Association, and interested himself deeply in details of missionary labours. Indeed, to the last day of his life, his thoughts often turned to foreign lands ; and one of the last notes he wrote was to the Secretary of the Association in Edinburgh, expressing his unabated interest in their prosperity.

During the first years of his college course, his studies did not absorb his whole attention ; but no sooner was the change on his soul begun, than his studies shared in the results. A deeper sense of responsibility led him to occupy his talents for the service of him who bestowed them. There have been few who, along with a devotedness of spirit that sought to be ever directly engaged in the Lord's work, have nevertheless retained such continued and undecaying esteem for the advantages of study. While attending the usual literary and philosophical classes, he found time to turn his attention to Geology and Natural History. And often in his days of most successful preaching, when, next to his own soul, his parish and his flock were his only care, he has been known to express a regret that he had not laid up in former days more stores of all useful knowledge; for he found himself able to use the jewels of the Egyptians in the service of Christ. His previous studies would sometimes flash into his mind some happy illustration of Divine truth, at the very moment when he was most solemnly applying the glorious gospel to the most ignorant and vile.

His own words will best show his estimate of study, and at the same time the prayerful manner in which he felt it should be carried on. "Do get on with your studies," he wrote to a young student in 1840. "Remember you are now forming the character of your future ministry in great measure, if God spare you. If you acquire slovenly or sleepy habits of study now, you will never get the better of it. Do everything in its own time. Do everything in earnest—if it is worth doing, then do it with all your might. Above all, keep much in the presence of God. Never see the face of man till you have seen his face who is our life, our all. Pray for others: pray for your teachers, fellow-students," &c. To another he wrote—"Beware of the atmosphere of the classics. It is pernicious indeed; and you need much of the south wind breathing over the Scriptures to counteract it. True, we ought to know them; but only as chemists handle poisons—to discover their qualities, not to infect their blood with them." And again—"Pray that the Holy Spirit would not only make you a believing and holy lad, but make you wise in your studies also. A ray of Divine light in the soul sometimes clears up a mathematical problem wonderfully. The smile of God calms the spirit, and the left hand of Jesus holds up the fainting head, and his Holy Spirit quickens the affection; so that even natural studies go on a million times more easily and comfortably."

Before entering the Divinity Hall, he had attended a private class for the study of Hebrew; and having afterwards attended the two sessions of Dr Brunton's College Class, he made much progress in that language. He could consult the Hebrew original of the Old Testament with as much ease as most of our ministers are able to consult the Greek of the New.

It was about the time of his first year's attendance at the Hall that I began to know him as an intimate friend. During the summer vacations—that we might redeem the time—some of us who remained in town, when most of our fellow-students were gone to the country, used to meet once every week in the forenoon, for the purpose of investigating some point of *Systematic Divinity*, and stating to each other the amount and result of our private reading. At another time we met in a similar way, till we had overtaken the chief points of the *Popish Controversy*. Advancement in our acquaintance with the Greek and Hebrew Scriptures also brought us together; and one summer the study of *Unfulfilled Prophecy* assembled a few of us once a week, at an early morning hour, when, though our views differed much on particular points, we never failed to get food to our souls in the Scriptures we explored. But no society of this kind was more useful and pleasant to us than one which, from its object, received the name of *Exegetical*. It met during the session of the Theological Classes every Saturday morning at half-past six. The study of Biblical criticism, and whatever might cast light on the Word of God, was our aim; and these meetings were kept up regularly during four sessions. Mr M'Cheyne spoke of himself as indebted to this society for much of that discipline of mind on Jewish literature and Scripture geography which was found to be so useful in the Mission of Inquiry to the Jews in after days.[1]

---

[1] The members of this Society were—Revs. *William Laughton*, now minister of St Thomas's, Greenock, in connection with the Free Church; *Thomas Brown*, Free Church, Kinneff; *William Wilson*, Free Church, Carmylie; *Horatius Bonar*, Free Church, Kelso; *Andrew A. Bonar*, Free Church, Collace; *Robert M. M'Cheyne*; *Alexander Somerville*, Free Church, Anderston, Glasgow; *John Thomson*, Mariners' Free Church, Leith; *Robert K. Hamilton*, Madras; *John Burne*, for some time at Madeira; *Patrick Borrowman*, Free Church, Glencairn; *Walter Wood*, Free Church, Westruther; *Henry Moncrieff*, Free Church, Kilbride; *James Cochrane*, Established Church, Cupar; *John Miller*, Secretary to Free Church Special Commission; *G. Smeaton*, Free Church, Auchterarder; *Robert Kinnear*, Free Church, Moffat; and *W. B. Clarke*, Free Church, Half-Morton. Every meeting was opened and closed with prayer. Minutes of the discussion were kept; and the Essays read were preserved in volumes. A very characteristic essay of Mr M'Cheyne's is, "Lebanon and its Scenery" (inserted in the Remains), wherein he adduces the evidence of travellers for facts and customs which himself was afterwards to see. Often in 1839, pleasant remembrances of these days of youthful study were suggested by what we actually witnessed; and in the essay referred to I find an interesting coincidence. He writes —"What a refreshing sight to his eye, yet undimmed with age, after resting forty years on the monotonous scenery of the desert, now to rest on Zion's olive-clad hills, and Lebanon, with its vine-clad base and

But these helps in study were all the while no more than supplementary. The regular systematic studies of the Hall furnished the main provision for his mental culture. Under Dr Chalmers for Divinity, and under Dr Welsh for Church History, a course of four years afforded no ordinary advantages for enlarging the understanding. New fields of thought were daily opened up. His notes and his diary testify that he endeavoured to retain what he heard, and that he used to read as much of the books recommended by the professors as his time enabled him to overtake. Many years after, he thankfully called to mind lessons that had been taught in these classes. Riding one day with Mr Hamilton (now of Regent Square, London) from Abernyte to Dundee, they were led to speak of the best mode of dividing a sermon. "I used," said he, "to despise Dr Welsh's rules at the time I heard him, but now I feel I *must use* them, for nothing is more needful for making a sermon memorable and impressive than a logical arrangement."

His intellectual powers were of a high order—clear and distinct apprehension of his subject, and felicitous illustration, characterized him among all his companions. To an eager desire for wide acquaintance with truth in all its departments, and a memory strong and accurate in retaining what he found, there was added a remarkable candour in examining what claimed to be the truth. He had also an ingenious and enterprising mind—a mind that could carry out what was suggested, when it did not strike out new light for itself. He possessed great powers of analysis; often his judgment discovered singular discrimination. His imagination seldom sought out objects of grandeur; for, as a friend has

overhanging forests, and towering peaks of snow." This was the very impression on our minds when we ourselves came up from the wilderness, as expressed in the Narrative, chap. ii.—"May 29. Next morning we saw at a distance a range of hills, running north and south, called by the Arabs *Djebel Khalie*. After wandering so many days in the wilderness, with its vast monotonous plains of level sand, the sight of these distant mountains was a pleasant relief to the eye; and we thought we could understand a little of the feeling with which Moses, after being forty years in the desert, would pray, 'I pray thee let me go over.' —DEUT. iii. 25."

39

truly said of him, "he had a kind and quiet eye, which found out the living and beautiful in nature, rather than the majestic and sublime."

He might have risen to high eminence in the circles of taste and literature, but denied himself all such hopes, that he might win souls. With such peculiar talents as he possessed, his ministry might have, in any circumstances, attracted many; but these attractions were all made subsidiary to the single desire of awakening the dead in trespasses and sins. Nor would he have expected to be blessed to the salvation of souls unless he had himself been a monument of sovereign grace. In his esteem, *"to be in Christ before being in the ministry"* was a thing indispensable. He often pointed to those solemn words of Jeremiah (xxiii. 21.), *"I have not sent these prophets, yet they ran; I have not spoken to them, yet they prophesied. But if they had stood in my counsel, and caused my people to hear my words, then they should have turned them from their evil way, and from the evil of their doings."*

It was with faith already in his heart that he went forward to the holy office of the ministry, receiving from his Lord the rod by which he was to do signs, and which, when it had opened rocks and made waters gush out, he never failed to replace upon the ark whence it was taken, giving glory to God! He knew not the way by which God was leading him; but even then he was under the guidance of the pillar-cloud. At this very period he wrote that hymn, *They sing the song of Moses*. His course was then about to begin; but now that it has ended, we can look back and plainly see that the faith he therein expressed was not in vain.

CHAPTER II

HIS LABOURS IN THE VINEYARD BEFORE ORDINATION

"He that goeth forth and weepeth, bearing precious seed, shall doubtless come again with rejoicing, bringing his sheaves with him."—Psa. cxxvi. 6.

WHILE he was still only undergoing a student's usual examinations before the Presbytery, in the spring and summer of 1835, several applications were made to him by ministers in the church, who desired to secure his services for their part of the vineyard. He was especially urged to consider the field of labour at Larbert and Dunipace, near Stirling, under Mr John Bonar, the pastor of these united parishes. This circumstance led him (as is often done in such cases) to ask the Presbytery of Edinburgh, under whose superintendence he had hitherto carried on his studies, to transfer the remainder of his public trials to another Presbytery, where there would be less press of business to occasion delay. This request being readily granted, his connection with Dumfriesshire led him to the Presbytery of Annan, who licensed him to preach the gospel on 1st July 1835. His feelings at the moment appear from a record of his own in the evening of the day: "Preached three probationary discourses in Annan Church, and, after an examination in Hebrew, was solemnly licensed to preach the gospel by Mr Monylaws, the Moderator. 'Bless the Lord, O my soul; and all that is within me be stirred up to praise and magnify his holy name!' What I have so long desired as the highest honour of man, thou at length givest me—me who dare scarcely use the words of Paul, 'Unto me who am less than the least of all saints is this grace given, that I should preach the unsearchable riches of Christ.' Felt somewhat solemnized, though unable to feel my unworthiness as I ought. Be clothed with humility."

An event occurred the week before which cast a solemniz-.

ing influence on him, and on his after fellow-traveller and brother in the gospel, who was licensed by another Presbytery that same day. This event was the lamented death of the Rev. John Brown Patterson, of Falkirk—one whom the Lord had gifted with pre-eminent eloquence and learning, and who was using all for his Lord, when cut off by fever. He had spoken much before his death of the awfulness of a pastor's charge, and his early death sent home the lesson to many, with the warning that the pastor's account of souls might be suddenly required of him.

On the following Sabbath Mr M'Cheyne preached for the first time, in Ruthwell Church, near Dumfries, on "the Pool of Bethesda"; and in the afternoon, on "the Strait Gate." He writes that evening in his diary: "Found it a more awfully solemn thing than I had imagined to announce Christ authoritatively; yet a glorious privilege!" The week after (Saturday July 11), "Lord, put me into thy service when and where thou pleasest. In thy hand all my qualities will be put to their appropriate end. Let me, then, have no anxieties." Next day, also, after preaching in St John's Church, Leith: "Remembered, before going into the pulpit, the confession which says[1] 'We have been more anxious about the messenger than the message.'" In preaching that day, he states, "It came across me in the pulpit, that if spared to be a minister, I might enjoy sweet flashes of communion with God in that situation. The mind is entirely wrought up to speak for God. It is possible, then, that more vivid acts of faith may be gone through then, than in quieter and sleepier moments."

It was not till the 7th of November that he began his labours at Larbert. In the interval, he preached in various places, and many began to perceive the peculiar sweetness of the word in his lips. In accepting the invitation to labour in the sphere proposed, he wrote: "It has always been my aim, and it is my prayer, to have *no plans* with regard to myself—

[1] He here refers to the *"Full and Candid Acknowledgment of Sin,"* for Students and Ministers, drawn up by the Commission of Assembly, 1651, and often reprinted since.

42

well assured as I am, that the place where the Saviour sees meet to place me, must ever be the best place for me."

The parish to which he had come was very large, containing six thousand souls. The parish church is at Larbert; but through the exertions of Mr Bonar, many years ago, a second church was erected for the people of Dunipace. Mr Hanna, afterwards minister of Stirling, had preceded Mr M'Cheyne in the duties of assistant in his field of labour; and Mr M'Cheyne now entered on it with a fully devoted and zealous heart, although in a weak state of health. As assistant, it was his part to preach every alternate Sabbath at Larbert and Dunipace, and during the week to visit among the population of both these districts, according as he felt himself enabled in body and soul. There was a marked difference between the two districts in their general features of character; but equal labour was bestowed on both by the minister and his assistant; and often did their prayer ascend that the windows of heaven might be opened over the two sanctuaries. Souls have been saved there. Often, however, did the faithful pastor mingle his tears with those of his younger fellow-soldier, complaining, "Lord, who hath believed our report?" There was much sowing in faith; nor was this sowing abandoned even when the returns seemed most inadequate.

Mr M'Cheyne had great delight in remembering that Larbert was one of the places where, in other days, that holy man of God, Robert Bruce, had laboured and prayed. Writing at an after period from the Holy Land, he expressed the wish, "May the spirit be poured upon Larbert as in Bruce's days." But more than all associations, the souls of the people, whose salvation he longed for, were ever present to his mind. A letter to Mr Bonar, in 1837, from Dundee, shews us his yearnings over them. "What an interest I feel in Larbert and Dunipace. It is like the land of my birth. Will the Sun of Righteousness ever rise upon it, making its hills and valleys bright with the light of the knowledge of Jesus!"

No sooner was he settled in his chamber here, than he commenced his work. With him, the commencement of all labour invariably consisted in the preparation of his own soul. The forerunner of each day's visitations was a calm season of private devotion during morning hours. The walls of his chamber were witnesses of his prayerfulness—I believe of his tears, as well as of his cries. The pleasant sound of psalms often issued from his room at an early hour. Then followed the reading of the Word for his own sanctification; and few have so fully realized the blessing of the first Psalm. His leaf did not wither, for his roots were in the waters. It was here, too, that he began to study so closely the works of Jonathan Edwards—reckoning them a mine to be wrought, and if wrought, sure to repay the toil. Along with this author, the *Letters of Samuel Rutherford* were often in his hand. Books of general knowledge he occasionally perused; but now it was done with the steady purpose of finding in them some illustration of spiritual truth. He rose from reading *Insect Architecture*, with the observation, "God reigns in a community of ants and ichneumons, as visibly as among living men or mighty seraphim!"

His desire to grow in acquaintance with Scripture was very intense; and both Old and New Testament were his regular study. He loved to range over the wide revelation of God. "He would be a sorry student of this world," said he to a friend, "who should for ever confine his gaze to the fruitful fields and well-watered gardens of this cultivated earth. He could have no true idea of what the world was, unless he had stood upon the rocks of our mountains and seen the bleak muirs and mosses of our barren land; unless he had paced the quarter-deck when the vessel was out of sight of land, and seen the waste of waters without any shore upon the horizon. Just so, he would be a sorry student of the Bible, who would not know all that God has inspired: who would not examine into the most barren chapters to collect the good for which they were intended; who would not strive to understand all the bloody battles which are chronicled, that he might find 'bread out of the eater, and honey out of the lion.'"—(June, 1836.)

His anxiety to have every possible help to holiness led him to notice what are the disadvantages of those who are not daily stirred up by the fellowship of more advanced believers.

"I have found, by some experience, that in the country here my watch does not go so well as it used to do in town. By small and gradual changes I find it either gains or loses, and I am surprised to find myself different in time from all the world, and, what is worse, from the sun. The simple explanation is, that in town I met with a steeple in every street, and a good-going clock upon it; and so any aberrations in my watch were soon noticed and easily corrected. And just so I sometimes think it may be with that inner watch, whose hands point not to time but to eternity. By gradual and slow changes the wheels of my soul lag behind, or the springs of passions become too powerful; and I have no living time-piece with which I may compare, and by which I may amend my going. You will say that I may always have the sun: And so it should be; but we have many clouds which obscure the sun from our weak eyes."—(Letter to Rev. H. Bonar, Kelso.)

From the first he fed others by what he himself was feeding upon. His teaching was in a manner the development of his soul's experience. It was a giving out of the inward life. He loved to come up from the pastures wherein the Chief Shepherd had met him—to lead the flock entrusted to his care to the spots where he found nourishment.

In the field of his labour, he found enough of work to overwhelm the Spirit. The several collieries and the Carron Iron-works furnish a population who are, for the most part, either sunk in deep indifference to the truth, or are opposed to it in the spirit of infidelity. Mr M'Cheyne at once saw that the pastor whom he had come to aid, whatever was the measure of his health, and zeal, and perseverance, had duties laid on him which were altogether beyond the power of man to overtake. When he made a few weeks' trial, the field appeared more boundless, and the mass of souls more impenetrable, than he had ever conceived.

It was probably, in some degree, his experience at this time that gave him such deep sympathy with the Church Extension Scheme, as a truly noble and Christian effort for bringing the glad tidings to the doors of a population who must otherwise remain neglected, and were themselves will-

45

ing so to live and die. He conveyed his impressions on this subject to a friend abroad, in the following terms:—"There is a soul-destroying cruelty in the cold-hearted opposition which is made to the multiplication of ministers in such neglected and over-grown districts as these. If one of our Royal Commissioners would but consent to undergo the bodily fatigue that a minister ought to undergo in visiting merely the sick and dying of Larbert (let alone the visitation of the whole, and preparation for the pulpit), and that for one month, I would engage that if he be able to rise out of his bed by the end of it, he would change his voice and manner at the Commission Board."

A few busy weeks passed over, occupied from morning to night in such cares and toils, when another part of the discipline he was to undergo was sent. In the end of December, strong oppression of the heart and an irritating cough caused some of his friends to fear that his lungs were affected; and for some weeks he was laid aside from public duty. On examination, it was found that though there was a dullness in the right lung, yet the material of the lungs was not affected. For a time, however, the air-vessels were so clogged and irritated, that if he had continued to preach, disease would have quickly ensued. But this also was soon removed, and, under cautious management, he resumed his work.

This temporary illness served to call forth the extreme sensitiveness of his soul to the responsibilities of his office. At its commencement—having gone to Edinburgh "in so sweet a sunshine morning that God seemed to have chosen it for him"—he wrote to Mr Bonar—"If I am not recovered before the third Sabbath, I fear I shall not be able to bear upon my conscience the responsibility of leaving you any longer to labour alone, bearing unaided the burden of 6000 souls. No, my dear Sir, I must read the will of God aright in his providence, and give way, when he bids me, to fresh and abler workmen. I hope and pray that it may be his will to restore me again to you and your parish, with a heart tutored by sickness to speak more and more as dying to dying." Then, mentioning two of the sick—"Poor A. D. and C. H., I often think of them. I can do no more for their good, except pray for them. Tell them that I do this without ceasing."

The days when a holy pastor, who knows the blood-sprinkled way to the Father, is laid aside, are probably as much a proof of the kindness of God to his flock as days of health and activity. He is occupied, during this season of retirement, in discovering the plagues of his heart, and in going in, like Moses, to plead with God face to face for his flock, and for his own soul. Mr M'Cheyne believed that God had this end in view with him; and that the Lord should thus deal with him at his entrance into the vineyard made him ponder these dealings the more. "Paul asked," says he, "What wilt thou have me *to do*?" and it was answered, "I will show him what great things he must *suffer* for my name's sake." Thus it may be with me. I have been too anxious to do great things. The lust of praise has ever been my besetting sin; and what more befitting school could be found for me than that of suffering alone, away from the eye and ear of man." Writing again to Mr Bonar, he tells him: "I feel distinctly that the whole of my labour during this season of sickness and pain, should be in the way of prayer and *intercession*. And yet, so strongly does Satan work in our deceitful hearts, I scarcely remember a season wherein I have been more averse to these duties. I try to 'build myself up in my most holy faith, praying in the Holy Ghost, keeping myself in the love of God, and looking for the mercy of the Lord Jesus unto eternal life.' That text of Jude has peculiar beauties for me at this season. If it be good to come under the love of God once, surely it is good to keep ourselves there. And yet how reluctant we are. I cannot doubt that boldness is offered me to enter into the holiest of all; I cannot doubt my right and title to enter continually by the new and bloody way; I cannot doubt that when I do enter in, I stand not only forgiven, but accepted in the Beloved; I cannot doubt that when I do enter in, the Spirit is willing and ready to descend like a dove, to dwell in my bosom as a Spirit of prayer and peace, enabling me to 'pray in the Holy Ghost;' and that Jesus is ready to rise up as my intercessor with the Father, praying for me though not for the world;

47

and that the prayer-hearing God is ready to bend his ear to requests which he delights to hear and answer. I cannot doubt that thus to dwell in God is the true blessedness of my nature; and yet, strange unaccountable creature! I am too often unwilling to enter in. I go about and about the sanctuary, and I sometimes press in through the rent vail, and see the blessedness of dwelling there to be far better than that of the tents of wickedness; yet it is certain that I do not dwell within."—"My prayers follow you, especially to the sick-beds of A. D. and C. H. I hope they still survive, and that Christ may yet be glorified in them."

On resuming his labours, he found a residence in Carron-vale. From this pleasant spot he used to ride out to his work. But pleasant as the spot was, yet being only partially re-covered, he was not satisfied; he lamented that he was unable to overtake what a stronger labourer would have accomplished. He often cast a regretful look at the collieries; and remembering them still at a later period, he reproached himself with neglect, though most unjustly. "The places which I left utterly unbroken in upon are Kinnaird and Milton. Both of these rise up against my conscience, particu-larly the last, through which I have ridden so often." It was not the comfort, but the positive usefulness of the ministry, that he envied; and he judged of places by their fitness to promote this great end. He said of a neighbouring parish, which he had occasion to visit—"The manse is altogether too sweet; other men could hardly live there without saying, 'This is my rest.' I don't think ministers' manses should ever be so beautiful."

A simple incident was overruled to promote the ease and fluency of his pulpit ministrations. From the very beginning of his ministry, he reprobated the custom of reading sermons, believing that to do so does exceedingly weaken the freedom and natural fervour of the messenger in delivering his message. Neither did he recite what he had written. But his custom was to impress on his memory the substance of what he had beforehand carefully written, and then to speak as he found liberty. One morning, as he rode rapidly along to Dunipace, his written sermons were dropped on the wayside.

This accident prevented him having the opportunity of preparing in his usual manner; but he was enabled to preach with more than usual freedom. For the first time in his life, he discovered that he possessed the gift of extemporaneous composition, and learned, to his own surprise, that he had more composedness of mind and command of language than he had believed. This discovery, however, did not in the least degree diminish his diligent preparation. Indeed, the only use that he made of the incident at the time it occurred was, to draw a lesson of dependence on God's own immediate blessing, rather than on the satisfactory preparation made. "One thing always fills the cup of my consolation, that God may work by the meanest and poorest words, as well as by the most polished and ornate—yea, perhaps more readily, that the glory may be all his own."

His hands were again full, distributing the bread of life in fellowship with Mr Bonar. The progress of his own soul, meanwhile, may be traced in some of the few entries that occur in his diary during this period :

"February 21. 1836—Sabbath.—Blessed be the Lord for another day of the Son of Man. Resumed my diary, long broken off; not because I do not feel the disadvantages of it —making you assume feelings and express rather what you wish to be than what you are—but because the advantages seem greater. It ensures sober reflection on the events of the day as seen in God's eye. Preached twice in Larbert, on the righteousness of God, Rom. i. 16. In the morning was more engaged in preparing the head than the heart. This has been frequently my error, and I have always felt the evil of it, especially in prayer. Reform it, then, O Lord."

Feb. 27.—Preached in Dunipace with more heart than ever I remember to have done, on Rom. v. 10, owing to the gospel nature of the subject and prayerful preparation. Audience smaller than usual! How happy and strange is the feeling when God gives the soul composure to stand and plead for him. O that it were altogether for him I plead, not for myself."

"March 5.—Preached in Larbert with very much comfort, owing chiefly to my remedying the error of 21st Feb. Therefore the heart and the mouth were full. 'Enlarge my heart, and I shall run,' said David. 'Enlarge my heart, and I shall preach'."

In this last remark we see the germ of his remarkably solemn ministry. His heart was filled, and his lips then spoke what he felt within his heart. He gave out not merely living water, but living water drawn at the springs that he had himself drank of; and is not this a true gospel ministry? Some venture to try what they consider a more *intellectual* method of addressing the conscience; but ere a minister attempts this mode, he ought to see that he is one who is able to afford more deep and anxious preparation of heart than other men. Since the intellectual part of the discourse is not that which is most likely to be an arrow in the conscience, those pastors who are intellectual men must bestow ten-fold more prayerfulness on their work, if they would have either their own or their people's souls affected under their word. If we are ever to preach with compassion for the perishing, we must ourselves be moved by those same views of sin and righteousness which moved the human soul of Jesus. (See Psalms xxxviii. and lv.)

About this time he occasionally contributed papers to the *Christian Herald*: one of these was *On sudden Conversions,* showing that Scripture led us to expect such. During this month, he seems to have written the "*Lines on Mungo Park,*" one of the pieces which attracted the notice of Professor Wilson. But whatever he engaged in, his aim was to honour his Master. I find him, after hearing a sermon by another, remarking (April 3rd), "Some things powerful; but I thirst to hear more of Christ."

On Sabbath, the 6th, he writes, "Preached with some tenderness of heart. O why should I not weep, as Jesus did over Jerusalem? Evening—Instructing two delightful Sabbath-schools. Much bodily weariness. Gracious kindness of God in giving rest to the weary."

"April 13.—Went to Stirling to hear Dr Duff once more upon his system. With greater warmth and energy than ever. He kindles as he goes. Felt almost constrained to go the whole length of his system with him. If it were only to raise up an audience, it would be defensible; but when it is to raise up teachers it is more than defensible. I am now made willing, if God shall open the way, to go to India. Here am I; send me!"

The missionary feeling in his soul continued all his life. The Lord had really made him willing; and this preparedness to go anywhere completed his preparation for unselfish, self-denied work at home. Must there not be somewhat of this missionary tendency in all true ministers? Is any one truly the Lord's messenger who is not quite willing to go when and where the Lord calls? Is it justifiable in any to put aside a call from the north, on the ground that he *wishes* one from the south? We must be found in the position of Isaiah, if we are to be really sent of God.

"April 24.—O that this day's labour may be blessed! and not mine alone, but all thy faithful servants all over the world, till *thy Sabbath* come."

"April 26.—Visiting in Carron-shore. Well received everywhere. Truly a pleasant labour. Cheered me much. Preached to them afterwards from Proverbs i."

"May 8.—Communion in Larbert. Served as an elder and help to the faithful. Partook with some glimpses of faith and joy. Served by a faithful old minister (Mr Dempster of Denny), one taught of God. This morning stood by the dying —evening, stood by the dead, poor J. F. having died last night. I laid my hand on her cold forehead, and tried to shut her eyes. Lord give me strength for living to thee!—strength also for a dying hour."

"May 15.—This day an annular eclipse of the sun. Kept both the services together in order to be in time. Truly a beautiful sight to see the shining edge of the sun all round the dark disc of the moon. Lord, one day thy hand shall put out those candles; for there shall be no need of the sun to lighten the happy land; the Lamb is the light thereof—a sun that cannot be eclipsed—that cannot go down."

"May 17.—Visited thirteen families, and addressed them all in the evening in the school, on Jeremiah l. 4, 'Going and weeping.' Experienced some enlargement of soul; said some plain things; and had some desire for their salvation, that God might be praised."

"May 21.—Preparation for the Sabbath. My birth-day. I have lived twenty-three years. Blessed be my Rock. Though I am a child in knowledge of my Bible and of Thee, yet use me for what a child can do, or a child can suffer. How few sufferings I have had in the year that is past, except in my own body. Oh! that as my day is my strength may be. Give me strength for a suffering and for a dying hour!"

"May 22.—O Lord, when thou workest, all discouragements vanish—when thou art away, any thing is a discouragement. Blessed be God for such a day—one of a thousand! O why not always this? Watch and pray."

Being in Edinburgh this month, during the sitting of the General Assembly, he used the opportunity of revisiting some of his former charge in the Canongate. "J. S., a far-off inquirer, but surely God is leading. His hand draws out these tears. Interesting visits to L.; near death, and still in the same mind. I cannot but hope that some faith is here. Saw Mrs M.; many tears: felt much, though I am still doubtful, and in the dark. Thou knowest, Lord!"

"June 11.—Yesterday up in Dunipace. It would seem as if I were afraid to name the name of Christ. Saw many worldly people greatly needing a word in season, yet could not get up my heart to speak. What I did failed almost completely. I am not worthy, Lord! To-day sought to prepare my heart for the coming Sabbath. After the example of Boston, whose life I have been reading, examined my heart with prayer and fasting. 1. Does my heart really close with the offer of salvation by Jesus? Is it my choice to be saved in the way which gives him all the praise, and me none? Do I not only see it to be the Bible way of salvation, but does it cordially approve itself to my heart as delightful? Lord search me and try me, for I cannot but answer, Yes, yes. 2. Is it the desire of my heart to be made altogether holy? Is there any sin I wish to retain? Is sin a grief to me, the sudden risings and overcomings thereof especially? Lord, thou knowest all things—thou knowest that I hate all sin, and desire to be made altogether *like thee*. It is the sweetest word

in the Bible—'Sin *shall not* have dominion over you.' O
then that I might lie low in the dust—the lower the better
—that Jesus' righteousness and Jesus' strength alone be
admired. Felt much deadness and much grief, that I cannot
grieve for this deadness. Towards evening revived. Got a
calm spirit through psalmody and prayer."

"June 12—Sabbath.—To-day a sinner preached Jesus,
the same Jesus who has done all things for him, and that
so lately! A day of much help, of some earnest looking-up of
the heart to that alone quickening power, of much temptation to flattery and pride. O for breathing gales of spiritual
life! Evening—Somewhat helped to lay Jesus before little
children in his beauty and excellency. Much fatigue, yet
some peace. Surely a day in thy courts is better than a
thousand."

"June 15.—Day of visiting—rather a happy one—in
Carron-shore. Large meeting in the evening. Felt very happy
after it, though mourning for *bitter speaking of the gospel*.
Surely it is a gentle message, and should be spoken with
angelic tenderness, especially by such a needy sinner."

Of this bitterness in preaching, he had little indeed in
after days; yet so sensible was he of its being quite natural
to all of us, that oftentimes he made it the subject of conversation, and used to grieve over himself if he had spoken with
anything less than solemn compassion. I remember on one
occasion, when we met, he asked what my last Sabbath's
subject had been. It had been, "The wicked shall be turned
into hell." On hearing this awful text, he asked, "Were you
able to preach it *with tenderness*?" Certain it is that the
tone of reproach and upbraiding is widely different from the
voice of solemn warning. It is not saying hard things that
pierces the consciences of our people; it is the voice of Divine
love heard amid the thunder. The sharpest point of the two-
edged sword is not *death* but *life*; and against self-righteous
souls this latter ought to be more used than the former. For
such souls can hear us tell of the open gates of hell and the
unquenchable fire far more unconcernedly than of the gates
of heaven wide-open for their immediate return. When we
preach that the glad tidings *were intended to impart imme-*

53

diate assurance of eternal life to every sinner that believes them, we strike deeper upon the proud enmity of the world to God, than when we show the eternal curse and the second death.

"June 19—Sabbath.—Wet morning. Preached at Dunipace to a small audience, on Parable of the Tares. I thank God for that blessed parable.——In both discourses I can look back on many hateful thoughts of pride, and self-admiration, and love of praise, stealing the heart out of the service."

"June 22.—Carron-shore. My last. Some tears; yet I fear some like the messenger, not the message; and I fear I am so vain as to love that love. Lord, let it not be so. Perish *my* honour, and let *Thine* be exalted for ever."

"June 26—True Sabbath-day. Golden sky. Full church, and more liveliness than sometimes. Shall I call the liveliness of this day a gale of the Spirit, or was all natural? I know that all was not of grace: the self-admiration, the vanity, the desire of honour, the bitterness—these were all breaths of earth or hell. But was there no grace? Lord, thou knowest. I dare not wrong thee by saying—No! Larbert Sabbath-school, with the same liveliness and joy. Domestic work with the same. Praised be God! O that the savour of it may last through the week! By this may I test if it be all of nature, or much of grace. Alas! how I tremble for my Monday mornings—these seasons of lifelessness. Lord, bless the seeds sown this day in the hearts of my friends, by the hand of my friends, and all over the world,—hasten the harvest!"

"July 3.—After a week of working and hurried preparation, a Sabbath of mingled peace and pain. Called, morning before preaching, to see Mrs E. dying. Preached on the Jailor—discomposedly—with some glimpses of the genuine truth as it is in Jesus. Felt there was much mingling of experience. At times the congregation was lightened up from their dull flatness, and then they sunk again into lethargy. O Lord, make me hang on thee to open their hearts, thou opener of Lydia's heart. I fear thou wilt not bless my preaching, until I am brought thus to hang on thee. O keep not back a blessing for my sin! Afternoon—On the Highway of the Redeemed,

54

with more ease and comfort. Felt the truth sometimes boiling up from my heart into my words. Some glimpses of tenderness, yet much less of that spirit than the last two Sabbaths. Again saw the dying woman. O when will I plead, with my tears and inward yearnings, over sinners! O, compassionate Lord, give me to know what manner of spirit I am of! give me thy gentle spirit, that neither strives nor cries. Much weariness, want of prayerfulness, and want of cleaving to Christ." Tuesday the 5th, being the anniversary of his licence to preach the Gospel, he writes:—"Eventful week: One year I have preached *Jesus*, have I? or myself? I have often preached myself also, but Jesus I have preached."

About this time he again felt the hand of affliction, though it did not continue long. Yet it was plain to him now that personal trouble was to be one of the ingredients of that experience which helped to give a peculiar tone to his ministry.

"July 8.—Since Tuesday have been laid up with illness. Set by once more for a season to feel my unprofitableness and cure my pride. When shall this self-choosing temper be healed? 'Lord, I will preach, run, visit, wrestle,' said I. 'No, thou shalt lie in thy bed and suffer,' said the Lord. To-day missed some fine opportunities of speaking a word for Christ. The Lord saw I would have spoken as much for my own honour as his, and, therefore, shut my mouth. *I see a man cannot be a faithful minister, until he preaches Christ for Christ's sake*—until he gives up striving to attract people to himself, and seeks only to attract them to Christ. Lord, give me this! To-night some glimpses of humbling; and, therefore, some wrestling in social prayer. But my prayers are scarcely to be called prayer." Then, in the evening, "This day my brother has been five years absent from the body and present with the Lord, and knows more and loves more than all earthly saints together. Till the Day break and the shadows flee away, turn, my Beloved!"

"July 10.—I fear I am growing more earthly in some things. To-day I felt a difficulty in bringing in spiritual conversation immediately after preaching, when my bosom should be burning. Excused myself from dining out from other than the grand reason; though checked and corrected myself. Evening—Insensibly slid into worldly conversation. Let these things be corrected in me, O Lord, by the heart being more filled with love to Jesus; and more ejaculatory prayer."

"July 17—Sabbath.—O that I may remember my own word this day : that the hour of communion is the hour for the foxes—the little foxes—to spoil the vine. Two things that defile this day in looking back, are love of praise running through all, and consenting to listen to worldly talk at all. O that these may keep me humble and be my burden, leading me to the cross. Then, Satan, thou wilt be outwitted!"

"July 19.—Died, this day, W. M'Cheyne, my cousin-german, Relief minister, Kelso. O how I repent of our vain controversies on Establishments when we last met, and that we spoke so little of Jesus! O that we had spoken more one to another! Lord, teach me to be always speaking as dying to dying."

"July 24.—Dunipace Communion.—Heard Mr Purves of Jedburgh preach, 'Therefore with joy shall ye draw water out of the wells of salvation.' The only way to come to ordinances, and to draw from the well, is to come with the matter of acceptance settled, believing God's anger to be turned away. Truly a precious view of the freeness of the gospel very refreshing. My soul needs to be roused much to apprehend this truth."

Above (July 3) he spoke of "mingling experience with the genuine truth as it is in Jesus." It is to this that he refers again, in the last paragraph. His deep acquaintance with the human heart and passions often led him to dwell at greater length, not only on those topics whereby the sinner might be brought to discover his guilt, but also on marks that would evidence a change, than on "the Glad Tidings." And yet he ever felt that these blessed tidings, addressed to souls in the very gall of bitterness, were the true theme of the minister of Christ; and never did he preach other than a full salvation ready for the chief of sinners. From the very first, also, he carefully avoided the error of those who rather speculate or doctrinize about the Gospel, than preach the Gospel itself. Is not the true idea of preaching that of one, like Ahimaaz, coming with all-important tidings, and intent on making these tidings known? Occupied with the facts he has to tell, he has no heart to speculate on mere abstractions; nay, he is apt to forget what language he employs, excepting so far as the very grandeur of the tidings gives a glow of eloquence to his words. The glorious fact, *"By this man is preached unto you the forgiveness of sins,"* is the burden of every sermon. The crier is sent to the openings of the gate by his Lord—to herald forth this one infinitely important truth through the whole creation under heaven.

He seems invariably to have applied for his personal benefit what he gave out to his people. We have already noticed how he used to feed on the Word, not in order to prepare himself for his people, but for personal edification. To do so was a fundamental rule with him; and all pastors will feel that, if they are to prosper in their own souls, they must so use the word—sternly refusing to admit the idea of feeding others, until satiated themselves. And for similar ends, it is needful that we let the truth we hear preached sink down into our own souls. We, as well as our people, must drink in the falling shower. Mr M'Cheyne did so. It is common to find him speaking thus:—"July 31, Sabbath—Afternoon, on Judas betraying Christ; much more tenderness than ever I felt before. O that I might abide in the bosom of him who washed Judas' feet, and dipped his hand in the same dish with him, and warned him, and grieved over him—that I might catch the infection of his love, of his tenderness, so wonderful, so unfathomable."

Coming home on a Sabbath evening (Aug. 7th) from Torwood Sabbath-school, a person met him who suggested an opportunity of usefulness. There were two families of gypsies encamped at Torwood, within his reach. He was weary with a long day's labour; but instantly, as was his custom on such a call, set off to find them. By the side of their wood-fire, he opened out the parable of the Lost Sheep, and pressed it on their souls in simple terms. He then knelt down in prayer for them, and left them somewhat impressed and very grateful.

At this time a youthful parishioner, for whose soul he felt

much anxiety, left his father's roof. Ever watchful for souls, he seized this opportunity of laying before him more fully the things belonging to his peace.

"My dear G——, You will be surprised to hear from me. I have often wished to be better acquainted with you; but in these sad parishes we cannot manage to know and be intimate with every one we would desire. And now you have left your father's roof and our charge; still my desires go after you, as well as the kind thoughts of many others; and since I cannot now speak to you, I take this way of expressing my thoughts to you. I do not know in what light you look upon me, whether as a grave and morose minister, or as one who might be a companion and friend; but, really, it is so short a while since I was just like you, when I enjoyed the games which you now enjoy, and read the books which you now read, that I never can think of myself as anything more than a boy. This is one great reason why I write to you. The same youthful blood flows in my veins that flows in yours—the same fancies and buoyant passions dance in my bosom as in yours—so that, when I would persuade you to come with me to the same Saviour, and to walk the rest of your life 'led by the Spirit of God,' I am not persuading you to anything beyond your years. I am not like a grey-headed grandfather—then you might answer all I say by telling me that you are a boy. No; I am almost as much a boy as you are; as fond of happiness and of life as you are; as fond of scampering over the hills, and seeing all that is to be seen, as you are.

"Another thing that persuades me to write you, my dear boy, is, that I have felt in my own experience the want of having a friend to direct and counsel me. I had a kind brother as you have, who taught me many things: he gave me a Bible, and persuaded me to read it; he tried to train me as a gardener trains the apple-tree upon the wall, but all in vain. I thought myself far wiser than he, and would always take my own way; and many a time, I well remember, I have seen him reading his Bible, or shutting his closet door

58

to pray, when I have been dressing to go to some frolic, or some dance of folly. Well, this dear friend and brother died; and though his death made a greater impression upon me than ever his life had done, still I found the misery of being *friendless*. I do not mean that I had no relations and worldly friends, for I had many; but I had no friend *who cared for my soul*. I had none to direct me to the Saviour—none to awaken my slumbering conscience—none to tell me about the blood of Jesus washing away all sin—none to tell me of the Spirit who is so willing to change the heart, and give the victory over passions. I had no minister to take me by the hand, and say, 'Come with me, and we will do thee good.' Yes, I had one friend and minister, but that was Jesus himself, and he led me in a way that makes me give him, and him only, all the praise. Now, though Jesus may do this again, yet the more common way with him is to use earthly guides. Now, if I could supply the place of such a guide to you, I should be happy. To be a finger-post is all that I want to be—pointing out the way. This is what I so much wanted myself—this is what you need not want, unless you wish.

"Tell me, dear G., would you work less pleasantly through the day—would you walk the streets with a more doleful step—would you eat your meat with less gladness of heart—would you sleep less tranquilly at night, if you had *the forgiveness of sins*—that is, if all your wicked thoughts and deeds—lies, thefts, and Sabbath-breakings—were all blotted out of God's book of remembrance? Would this make you less happy do you think? You dare not say it would. But would the forgiveness of sins not make you more happy than you are? Perhaps you will tell me that you are very happy as you are. I quite believe you. I know that I was very happy when I was unforgiven. I know that I had great pleasure in many sins—in Sabbath-breaking for instance. Many a delightful walk I have had—speaking my own words, thinking my own thoughts, and seeking my own pleasure on God's holy day. I fancy few boys were ever happier in an unconverted state than I was. No sorrow clouded my brow —no tears filled my eyes, unless over some nice story-book; so that I know that you say quite true, when you say that you are happy as you are. But ah! is not this just the saddest thing of all, that you should be happy whilst you are a child of wrath—that you should smile, and eat, and drink, and be merry, and sleep sound, when this very night you may be in *hell*! Happy while unforgiven!— a terrible happiness. It is like the Hindoo widow who sits upon the funeral pile with her dead husband, and sings songs of joy when they are setting fire to the wood with which she is to be burned. Yes, you may be quite happy in this way, till you die, my boy; but when you look back from hell, you will say, it was a miserable kind of happiness. Now, do you think it would not give you more happiness to be forgiven—to be able to put on Jesus, and say, 'God's anger is turned away?' Would not you be happier at work, and happier in the house, and happier in your bed? I can assure you, from all that ever I have felt of it, the pleasures of being forgiven are as superior to the pleasures of an unforgiven man, as heaven is higher than hell. The peace of being forgiven reminds me of the calm, blue sky, which no earthly clamours can disturb. It lightens all labour, sweetens every morsel of bread, and makes a sick bed all soft and downy—yea, it takes away the scowl of death. Now, forgiveness may be yours *now*. It is not given to those who are good. It is not given to any because they are less wicked than others. It is given *only* to those who, feeling that their sins have brought a curse on them which they cannot lift off, 'look unto Jesus,' as bearing all away.

"Now, my dear boy, I have no wish to weary you. If you are anything like what I was, you will have yawned many a time already over this letter. However, if the Lord deal graciously with you, and touch your young heart, as I pray he may, with a desire to be forgiven, and to be made a child of God, perhaps you will not take ill what I have written to you in much haste. As this is the first time you have been away from home, perhaps you have not learned to write letters yet; but if you have, I would like to hear from you, how you come on—what convictions you feel, if you feel any —what difficulties—what parts of the Bible puzzle you; and then I would do my best to unravel them. You read your Bible regularly, of course; but do try and understand it, and still more, to *feel* it. Read more parts than one at a time. For example, if you are reading Genesis, read a Psalm also; or, if you are reading Matthew, read a small bit of an epistle also. *Turn the Bible into prayer.* Thus, if you were reading the 1st Psalm, spread the Bible on the chair before you, and kneel and pray, 'O Lord, give me the blessedness of the man,' &c. 'Let me not stand in the counsel of the ungodly,' &c. This is the best way of knowing the meaning of the Bible, and of learning to pray. In prayer confess your sins by name —going over those of the past day one by one. Pray for your friends by name—father, mother, &c. &c. If you love them, surely you will pray for their souls. I know well that there are prayers constantly ascending for you from your own house; and will you not pray for them back again? Do this regularly. If you pray sincerely for others, it will make you pray for yourself.

"But I must be done. Good bye, dear G. Remember me to your brother kindly, and believe me your sincere friend,

"R. M. M."

It is the shepherd's duty (Ezek. xxxiv. 4), in visiting his flock, to discriminate; "strengthening the diseased, healing that which was sick, binding up that which was broken, bringing again that which was driven away, seeking that which was lost." This Mr M'Cheyne tried to do. In an after-letter to Mr Somerville, of Anderston, in reference to the people of these parishes, whom he had had means of knowing, he wrote, "Take more heed to the saints than ever I did. Speak a word in season to S. M. S. H. will drink in simple truth, but tell him to be humble-minded. Cause L. H. to learn in silence; speak not of *religion* to her, but speak to her case always. Teach A. M. to look simply at Jesus. J. A. warn and teach. Get worldliness from the B.'s, if you can. Mrs G. awake, or keep awake. Speak faithfully to the B.'s. Tell me of M. C., if she is really a believer, and grows. A. K., has the light visited her? M. T. I have had some doubts of. M. G. lies sore upon my conscience; I did no good to that woman; she always managed to speak of *things about the*

61

truth. Speak boldly. What matter in eternity the slight awkwardness of time!"

It was about this time that the managers and congregation of the new church, St Peter's, Dundee, invited him to preach as one of the candidates; and, in the end of August, chose him to be their pastor, with one accord. He accepted the call under an awful sense of the work that lay before him. He would rather, he said, have made choice for himself of such a rural parish as Dunipace; but the Lord seemed to desire it otherwise. "His ways are in the sea." More than once, at a later period, he would say, "We might have thought that God would have sent a strong man to such a parish as mine, and not a feeble reed."

The first day he preached in St Peter's as a candidate (August 14th), is thus recorded : "Forenoon—Mind not altogether in a preaching frame; on the Sower. Afternoon— With more encouragement and help of the Spirit; on the Voice of the Beloved, in Cant. ii. 8-17.[1] In the Evening— With all my heart; on *Ruth*. Lord, keep me humble." Returning from St Peter's, the second time, he observed in his class of girls at Dunipace more than usual anxiety. One of them seemed to be thoroughly awakened that evening. "Thanks be to thee, Lord, for anything," he writes that evening; for as yet he had sown without seeing fruit. It seems to have been part of the Lord's dealing with him, thus to teach him to persevere in duty and in faith, even where there was no obvious success. The arrow that was yet to wound hundreds was then receiving its point; but it lay in the quiver for a time. The Lord seemed to be touching his own heart and melting it by what he spoke to others, rather than touching or melting the hearts of those he spoke to. But from the day of his preaching in St Peter's, tokens of success began. His first day there, especially the evening sermon on Ruth, was blessed to two souls in Dundee; and now he sees souls begin to melt under his last words in the parish where he thought he had hitherto spent his strength in vain.

As he was now to leave this sphere, he sought out with deep anxiety a labourer who would help their overburdened

---

[1] See this characteristic sermon in the *Remains*.

pastor, in true love to the people's souls. He believed he had found such a labourer in Mr Somerville, his friend who had shared his every thought and feeling in former days, and who, with a sharp sickle in his hand, was now advancing toward the harvest field. "I see plainly," he wrote to Mr Bonar, "that my poor attempts at labour in your dear parish will soon be eclipsed. But if at length the iron front of unbelief give way, if the hard faces become furrowed with the tears of anxiety and of faith, under whatever ministry, you will rejoice, and I will rejoice, and the angels, and the Father and God of angels, will rejoice." It was in this spirit that he closed his short ten months of labour in this region.

His last sermons to the people of Larbert and Dunipace were on Hosea xiv. I, "O Israel, return unto the Lord thy God;" and Jeremiah viii. 20, "Harvest is past." In the evening he writes, "Lord, I feel bowed down because of the little I have done for them which thou mightest have blessed! My bowels yearn over them, and all the more that I have done so little. Indeed I might have done ten times as much as I have done. I might have been in every house; I might have spoken always as a minister. Lord, canst thou bless partial, unequal efforts?"

I believe it was about this time that some of us first of all began our custom of praying specially for each other on Saturday evening, with a reference to our engagements in the ministry next day. This concert for prayer we have never since seen cause to discontinue. It has from time to time been widened in its circle; and as yet his has been the only voice that has been silenced of all that thus began to go in on each other's behalf before the Lord. Mr M'Cheyne never failed to remember this time of prayer. "Larbert and Dunipace are always on my heart, especially on the Saturday evenings, when I pray for a glorious Sabbath!" On one occasion, in Dundee, he was asked if the accumulation of business in his parish never led him to neglect the season of prayer on a busy Saturday. His reply was, that he was not aware that it ever did. "What would my people do if I were not to pray?"

So steady was he in Sabbath preparations, from the first

day to the last time he was with them, that though at prayer meetings, or similar occasions, he did not think it needful to have much laid up before coming to address his people, yet, anxious to give them on the Sabbath what had cost him somewhat, he never, without an urgent reason, went before them without much previous meditation and prayer. His principle on this subject was embodied in a remark he made to some of us who were conversing on the matter. Being asked his view of diligent preparation for the pulpit, he reminded us of Exodus xxvii. 20. "*Beaten oil—beaten oil for the lamps of the sanctuary.*" And yet his prayerfulness was greater still. Indeed, he could not neglect fellowship with God before entering the congregation. He needed to be bathed in the love of God. His ministry was so much a bringing out of views that had first sanctified his own soul, that the healthiness of his soul was absolutely needful to the vigour and power of his ministrations.

During these ten months the Lord had done much for him, but it was chiefly in the way of discipline for a future ministry. He had been taught a minister's heart; he had been tried in the furnace; he had tasted deep personal sorrow, little of which has been recorded; he had felt the fiery darts of temptation; he had been exercised in self-examination and in much prayer; he had proved how flinty is the rock, and had learnt that in lifting the rod by which it was to be smitten, success lay in Him alone who enabled him to lift it up. And thus prepared of God for the peculiar work that awaited him, he turned his face towards Dundee, and took up his abode in the spot where the Lord was so marvellously to visit him in his ministry.

CHAPTER III

FIRST YEARS OF LABOUR
IN DUNDEE

*"Ye know, from the first day that I came into Asia, after
what manner I have been with you at all seasons, serving the
Lord with all humility of mind, and with many tears and
temptations."*—ACTS xx. 18-19.

THE day on which he was ordained pastor of a flock was a
day of much anxiety to his soul. He had journeyed by Perth
to spend the night preceding under the roof of his kind
friend Mr Grierson, in the manse of Errol. Next morning,
ere he left the manse, three passages of Scripture occupied
his mind. 1. *"Thou wilt keep him in perfect peace whose
mind is stayed on thee; because he trusteth in thee."* Isaiah
xxvi. 3. This verse was seasonable; for, as he sat meditating
on the solemn duties of the day, his heart trembled. 2. *"Give
thyself wholly to these things."* 1 Tim. iv. 15. May that word
(he prayed) sink deep into my heart. 3. *"Here am I, send me."*
Isaiah vi. 8. "To go, or to stay—to be here till death, or to
visit foreign shores— whatsoever, wheresoever, whensoever
thou pleasest." He rose from his knees with the prayer,
"Lord, may thy grace come with the laying on of the hands
of the Presbytery."

He was ordained on November 24. 1836. The service
was conducted by Mr Roxburgh of St John's, through whose
exertions the new church had been erected, and who ever
afterwards cherished the most cordial friendship towards
him. On the Sabbath following, he was introduced to his
flock by Mr John Bonar of Larbert, with whom he had
laboured as a son in the Gospel. Himself preached in the
afternoon upon Isaiah lxi 1-3, *"The Spirit of the Lord is upon
me,"* &c.—of which he writes, "May it be prophetic of the
object of my coming here!" And truly it was so. That very
sermon—the first preached by him as a pastor—was the

means of awakening souls, as he afterwards learnt; and ever onward the impressions left by his words seemed to spread and deepen among his people. To keep up the remembrance of this solemn day, he used in all the subsequent years of his ministry to preach from this same text on the anniversary of his ordination.[1] In the evening of that day, Mr Bonar again preached on "*These times of refreshing.*" "A noble sermon, showing the marks of such times. Ah! when shall we have them here? Lord bless this word, to help their coming! Put thy blessing upon this day! Felt given over to God, as one bought with a price."

There was a rapid growth in his soul, perceptible to all who knew him well, from this time. Even his pulpit preparations, he used to say, became easier from this date. He had earnestly sought that the day of his ordination might be a time of new grace; he expected it would be so; and there was a peculiar work to be done by his hands, for which the Holy Spirit did speedily prepare him.

His diary does not contain much of his feelings during his residence in Dundee. His incessant labours left him little time, except what he scrupulously spent in the direct exercises of devotion. But what we have seen of his manner of study and self-examination at Larbert, is sufficient to show in what a constant state of cultivation his soul was kept; and his habits in these respects continued with him to the last. Jeremy Taylor recommends—"If thou meanest to enlarge thy religion, do it rather by enlarging thine ordinary devotions than thy extraordinary." This advice describes very accurately the plan of spiritual life on which Mr M'Cheyne acted. He did occasionally set apart seasons for special prayer and fasting, occupying the time so set apart exclusively in devotion. But the real secret of his soul's prosperity lay in the daily enlargement of his heart in fellowship with his God. And the river deepened as it flowed on to eternity; so that he at least reached that feature of a holy pastor which Paul pointed out to Timothy (iv. 15)—"His profiting did appear to all."

[1] "The Acceptable Year of the Lord" was one of these Anniversary Sermons, preached November 1840.

In his own house everything was fitted to make you feel that the service of God was a cheerful service, while he sought that every arrangement of the family should bear upon eternity. His morning hours were set apart for the nourishment of his own soul; not, however, with the view of laying up a stock of grace for the rest of the day—for manna will corrupt if laid by—but rather with the view of "giving the eye the habit of looking upward all the day, and drawing down gleams from the reconciled countenance." He was sparing in the hours devoted to sleep, and resolutely secured time for devotion before breakfast, although often wearied and exhausted when he laid himself to rest. "A soldier of the cross," was his remark, "must endure hardness." Often he sang a Psalm of praise, as soon as he arose, to stir up his soul. Three chapters of the Word was his usual morning portion. This he thought little enough, for he delighted exceedingly in the Scriptures: they were better to him than thousands of gold or silver. "When you write," said he to a friend, "tell me the meaning of Scriptures." To another, in expressing his value for the Word, he said, "One gem from that ocean is worth all the pebbles of earthly streams."

His chief season of relaxation seemed to be breakfast-time. He would come down with a happy countenance and a full soul; and after the sweet season of family prayer, forthwith commence forming plans for the day. When he was well, nothing seemed to afford him such true delight as to have his hands full of work. Indeed, it was often remarked that in him you found—what you rarely meet with— a man of high poetic imagination and deep devotion, who nevertheless was engaged unceasingly in the busiest and most laborious activities of his office.

His friends could observe how much his soul was engrossed during his times of study and devotion. If interrupted on such occasions, though he never seemed ruffled, yet there was a kind of gravity and silence that implied—"I wish to be alone." But he further aimed at enjoying God *all the day*. And referring on one occasion to those blank hours which so often are a believer's burden—hours during which the soul is dry and barren—he observed, "They are proofs of

67

how little we are *filled* with the presence of God, how little we are *branch-like* [1] in our faith."

This careful attention to the frame of his spirit did not hinder his preparation for his people: on the contrary, it kept alive his deep conscientiousness, and kept his warm compassion ever yearning. When asked to observe a Saturday as a day of fasting and prayer, along with some others who had a special object in view, he replied—"Saturday is an awkward day for ministers; for though I love to seek help from on High, I love also diligently to set my thoughts in order for the Sabbath. I sometimes fear that you fail in this latter duty."

During his first years in Dundee, he often rode out in an afternoon to the ruined church of Invergowrie, to enjoy an hour's perfect solitude; for he felt meditation and prayer to be the very sinews of his work. Such notices, also, as the following shew his systematic pursuit of personal holiness:

"April 9. 1837—Evening.—A very pleasant quietness. Study of the Epistle to the Hebrews. Came to a more intelligent view of the first six chapters than ever before. Much refreshed by John Newton; instructed by Edwards. Help and freedom in prayer. Lord, what a happy season is a Sabbath evening! What will Heaven be!"

"April 16—Sabbath Evening.—Much prayer and peace. Reading the Bible only."

"June 2.—Much peace and rest to-night. Much broken under a sense of my exceeding wickedness, which no eye can see but thine. Much persuasion of the sufficiency of Christ, and of the constancy of his love. O how sweet to work all day for God, and then to lie down at night under his smiles."

"June 17. 1838.—At Dumbarney communion. Much sin and coldness two days before. Lay low at his feet; found peace only in Jesus."

"September 25.—Spent last week at Blairgowrie; I hope not in vain. Much sin, weakness, and uselessness; much delight in the Word also, while opening it up at family prayer. May God make the Word fire. Opened 1 Thessalonians, the whole; enriching to my own mind. How true

[1] Compare Zechariah iv. 12, with John xv. 5.

68

is Psalm i.; yet observed in my heart a strange proneness to be entangled with the affairs of this life; not strange because I am good, but because I have been so often taught that bitterness is the end of it."

"Sept. 28.—Devoted chief part of Friday to fasting. Humbled and refreshed."

"Sept. 30—Sabbath.—Very happy in my work. Too little prayer in the morning. Must try to get early to bed on Saturday, that I may 'rise a great while before day.' " These early hours of prayer on Sabbath he endeavoured to have all his life; not for study, but for prayer. He never laboured at his sermons on a Sabbath. That day he kept for its original end, the *refreshment of his soul*. (Exodus, xxxi. 17.)

The parish of St Peter's, to which he had come, was large and very destitute. It is situated at the west end of the town, and included some part of the adjacent country. The church was built in connection with the Church Extension Scheme. The parish was a *quoad sacra* parish, detached from St John's. It contains a population of 4000 souls, very many of whom never crossed the threshold of any sanctuary. His congregation amounted, at the very outset, to about 1100 hearers, one-third of whom came from distant parts of the town.

Here was a wide field for parochial labour. It was also a very dead region—few, even of those who were living Christians, breathed their life on others; for the surrounding mass of impenetrable heathenism had cast its sad influence even over them. His first impressions of Dundee were severe. "A city given to idolatry and hardness of heart. I fear there is much of what Isaiah speaks of, 'The prophets prophesy lies, and the people love to have it so.' "

His first months of labour were very trying. He was not strong in bodily health, and that winter a fatal influenza prevailed for two or three months, so that most of his time in his parish was spent in visiting the sick and dying. In such cases he was always ready. "Did I tell you of the boy I was asked to see on Sabbath evening, just when I had got myself comfortably seated at home? I went and was speaking to him of the freeness and fullness of Jesus, when he gasped a little and died."

In one of his first visits to the sick, the narrative of the Lord's singular dealings with one of his parishioners greatly encouraged him to carry the glad tidings to the distressed under every disadvantage. Four years before, a young woman had been seized with cholera, and was deprived of the use of speech for a whole year. The Bible was read to her, and men of God used to speak and pray with her. At the end of the year her tongue was loosed, and the first words heard from her lips were praise and thanksgiving for what the Lord had done for her soul. It was in her chamber he was now standing, hearing from her own lips what the Lord had wrought.

On another occasion, during the first year of his ministry, he witnessed the death-bed conversion of a man who, till within a few days of his end, almost denied that there was a God. This solid conversion, as he believed it to be, stirred him up to speak with all hopefulness, as well as earnestness, to the dying.

But it was, above all, to the children of God that his visitations seemed blessed. His voice, and his very eye, spoke tenderness; for personal affliction had taught him to feel sympathy with the sorrowing. Though the following be an extract from a letter, yet it will be recognized by many as exhibiting his mode of dealing with God's afflicted ones in his visitations: "There is a sweet word in Exodus (iii. 7), which was pointed out to me the other day by a poor bereaved child of God—'I know their sorrows.' Study that; it fills the soul. Another word like it is in Psalm ciii. 14—'He knoweth our frame.' May your own soul, and that of your dear friends, be fed by these things. A dark hour makes Jesus bright. Another sweet word—'They knew not that it was Jesus.'"

I find some specimens of his sick visits among his papers, noted down at a time when his work had not grown upon his hands. "January 25. 1837—Visited Mgt. M'Bain, a young woman of twenty-four, long ill of decline. Better or worse these ten years past. Spoke of *The one thing needful*,'

70

plainly. She sat quiet. February 14th—Had heard she was better—found her near dying. Spoke plainly and tenderly to her, commending Christ. Used many texts. She put out her hand kindly on leaving. 15th.—Still dying-like; spoke as yesterday. She never opened her eyes. 16th—Shewed her the dreadfulness of wrath; freeness of Christ; the majesty, justice, truth of God. Poor M. is fast going the way whence she shall not return. Many neighbours also always gather in. 17th—Read Psalm xxii.; shewed the sufferings of Christ; how sufficient an atonement; how feeling a high priest. She breathed loud, and groaned through pain. Died this evening at seven. I hardly ever heard her speak anything; and I will hope that thou art with Christ in glory, till I go and see. 20th—Prayed at her funeral. Saw her laid in St Peter's churchyard, *the first laid there,* by her own desire, in the fresh mould where never man was laid. May it be a token that she is with Him who was laid in a new tomb."

He records another case: "January 4. 1837—Sent for to Mrs S——. Very ill; asthmatic. Spoke on *'No condemnation to them that are in Christ.'* She said, 'But am I in Christ?' seemingly very anxious. Said she had often been so, and had let it go by. 5th—Still living; spoke to her of Christ, and of full salvation. (Myself confined in the house till the 16th.) 16th—Much worse. Not anxious to hear, yet far from rest. Dark, uneasy eye. Asked me, 'What is it to believe?' Spoke to her on *'God, who made light shine out of darkness.'* She seemed to take up nothing. Lord help! 17th—Still worse; wearing away. No smile; no sign of inward peace. Spoke of *'Remember me.'* Went over the whole gospel in the form of personal address. She drowsy. 18th—Quieter. *'My Lord and my God.'* She spoke at intervals. More cheerful; anxious that I should not go without prayer. Has much knowledge; complete command of the Bible. 19th—Spoke on *'Convincing of sin and righteousness.'* Rather more heart to hear. 20th—Psalm li. Her look and her words were lightsome. 23rd—Faintish and restless; no sign of peace. *'I am the way,'* and Psalm xxv. 24th—Still silent and little sign of anything. 26th—Psalm xl. *'The fearful pit.'* Very plain. Could not get anything out of her. February 1st—Died at twelve noon; no visible mark of light, or comfort, or hope. The day shall declare it."

One other case: "February 5. 1839.—Called suddenly in the evening. Found him near death. Careless family. Many round him. Spoke of the freeness and sufficiency of Jesus, *'Come unto me,'* &c., and *'The wrath of God revealed from heaven.'* Told him he was going where he would see Christ; asked him if he would be his Saviour? He seemed to answer; his father said, 'He is saying, yes.' But it was the throe of death. One or two indescribable gasps, and he died! I sat silent, and let God preach. 7th—Spoke of the *'Widow of Nain,'* and *'Behold, I stand at the door.'*"

Attendance at funerals was often to him a season of much exercise. Should it not be to all ministers a time for solemn inquiry? Was I faithful with this soul? Could this soul have learnt salvation from me every time I saw him? And did I pray as fervently as I spoke? And if we have tender pity for souls, we will sometimes feel as Mr M'Cheyne records: "September 24.— "Buried A. M. Felt bitterly the word, 'If any man draw back,' &c. Never had more bitter feelings at any funeral."

All who make any pretension to the office of shepherds visit their flocks;[1] yet there is a wide difference in the kind of visits which shepherds give. One does it formally, to discharge his duty and to quiet conscience; another makes it his delight. And of those who make it their delight, one goes forth on the regular plan of addressing all in somewhat of the same style; while another speaks freely, according as the wounds of his sheep come to view. On all occasions, this difficult and trying work must be gone about with a full heart, if it is to be gone about successfully at all. There is little in it to excite, for there is not the presence of numbers, and the few you see at a time are in their calmest, every-day mood. Hence there is need of being full of grace, and need of feeling as though God did visit every hearer by your

---

[1] Baxter (*Reformed Pastor*) says, "I dare prognosticate from knowledge of the nature of true grace, that all godly ministers will make conscience of this duty, and address themselves to it, unless they be, by some extraordinary accident, disabled."

means. Our object is not to get duty done, but to get souls saved. 2 Cor. xiii. 7. Mr M'Cheyne used to go forth in this spirit; and often after visiting from house to house for several hours, he would return to some room in the place in the evening, and preach to the gathered families. "September 26. 1838. Good visiting-day. Twelve families; many of them go nowhere. It is a great thing to be well furnished by meditation and prayer before setting out; it makes you a far more full and faithful witness. Preached in A. F.'s house on Job, '*I know that my Redeemer liveth.*' Very sweet and precious to myself."

Partly from his state of health, and partly from the vast accumulation of other labours, and the calls made on him for evangelizing elsewhere, he was never able to overtake the visitation of the whole district assigned him. He was blessed to attract and reclaim very many of the most degraded; and by Sabbath-schools, and a regular eldership, to take superintendence of the population, to a great extent. Still he himself often said that his parish had never fully shared in the advantages that attend an aggressive system of parochial labour. Once, when spending a day in the rural parish of Collace, as we went in the afternoon from door to door, and spoke to the children whom we met on the road-side, he smiled and said, "Well, how I envy a country minister; for he can get acquainted with his people, and have some insight into their real character." Many of us thought that he afterwards erred, in the abundant frequency of his evangelistic labours at a time when he was still bound to a particular flock.

He had an evening-class every week for the young people of his congregation. The Catechism and the Bible were his text books, while he freely introduced all manner of useful illustrations. He thought himself bound to prepare diligently for his classes, that he might give accurate and simple explanations, and unite what was interesting with the most solemn and awakening views. But it was his class for young communicants that engaged his deepest care, and wherein he saw most success. He began a class of this kind previous to his first Communion, and continued to form it again some weeks before every similar occasion. His tract, published in 1840 *"This do in remembrance of me,"* may be considered as exhibiting the substance of his solemn examinations on these occasions.

He usually noted down his first impressions of his communicants, and compared these notes with what he afterwards saw in them. Thus: "M. K., sprightly and lightsome, yet sensible; she saw plainly that the converted alone should come to the Table, but stumbled at the question, If she were converted? Yet she claimed being awakened and brought to Christ." Another: "Very staid, intelligent-like person, with a steady kind of anxiety, but, I fear, no feeling of helplessness. Thought that sorrow and prayer would obtain forgiveness. Told her plainly what I thought of her case." Another: "Knows she was once Christless; now she reads and prays, and is anxious. I doubt not there is some anxiety, yet I fear it may be only a self-reformation to recommend herself to God and to man. Told her plainly." "A. M., I fear much for him. Gave him a token with much anxiety; warned him very much." "C. P. does not seem to have any work of anxiety. He reads prayer-books, &c. Does not pray in secret. Seems not very intelligent."

He sought to encourage Sabbath-schools in all the districts of his parish. The hymn, *"Oil for the Lamp,"* was written to impress the parable on a class of Sabbath scholars in 1841. Some of his sweet, simple tracts were written for these schools. *"Reasons why Children should fly to Christ"* was the first, written at the New Year, 1839; and *"The Lambs of the Flock"* was another at a later period. His heart felt for the young. One evening, after visiting some of his Sabbath-schools, he writes: "Had considerable joy in teaching the children. O for real heart-work among them!" He could accommodate himself to their capacities; and he did not reckon it vain to use his talents in order to attract their attention; for he regarded the soul of a child as infinitely precious. Ever watchful for opportunities, on the blank leaf of a book which he had sent to a little boy of his congregation, he wrote these simple lines:—

Peace be to thee, gentle boy!
Many years of health and joy!
Love your Bible more than play—
Grow in wisdom every day.
Like the lark on hovering wing,
Early rise, and mount and sing;
Like the dove that found no rest
Till it flew to Noah's breast,
Rest not in this world of sin,
Till the Saviour take thee in.

He had a high standard in his mind as to the moral qualifications of those who should teach the young. When a
female teacher was sought for to conduct an evening school
in his parish for the sake of the mill-girls, he wrote to one
interested in the cause—"The qualifications she should possess for sewing and knitting, you will understand far better
than I. She should be able to keep up in her scholars the
fluency of reading, and the knowledge of the Bible and Catechism, which they may have already acquired. She should
be able to teach them to sing the praises of God, with feeling
and melody. But, far above all, she should be a Christian
woman, not in name only, but in deed and in truth—one
whose heart has been touched by the Spirit of God, and who
can love the souls of little children. Any teacher who wanted
this last qualification, I would look upon as a curse rather
than a blessing—a centre of blasting, and coldness, and
death, instead of a centre from which life, and warmth, and
heavenly influence might emanate."

It was very soon after his ordination that he began his
weekly prayer-meeting in the church. He had heard how
meetings of this kind had been blessed in other places, and
never had he any cause to regret having set apart the Thursday evening for this holy purpose. One of its first effects was
to quicken those who had already believed; they were often
refreshed upon these occasions even more than on the Sabbath. Some of the most solemn seasons of his ministry were
at those meetings. At their commencement, he wrote to me
an account of his manner of conducting them—"I give my
people a Scripture to be hidden in the heart—generally a
promise of the Spirit or the wonderful effects of his outpour-

ing.[1] I give them the heads of a sermon upon it for about twenty minutes. Prayer goes before and follows. Then I read some history of Revivals, and comment in passing. I think the people are very much interested in it: a number of people come from all parts of the town. But, oh! I need much the living Spirit to my own soul; I want my life to be hid with Christ in God. At present there is too much hurry, and bustle and outward working, to allow the calm working of the Spirit on the heart. I seldom get time to meditate, like Isaac, at evening-tide, except when I am tired; but the dew comes down when all nature is at rest—when every leaf is still."

A specimen of the happy freedom and familiar illustrations which his people felt to be peculiar to these meetings, may be found in the notes taken by one of his hearers, of *"Expositions of the Epistles to the Seven Churches,"* given during the year 1838. He had himself great delight in the Thursday evening meetings. "They will doubtless be remembered in eternity with songs of praise," said he, on one occasion; and at another time, observing the tender frame of a soul which was often manifested at these seasons, he said, "There is a stillness to the last word—not as on Sabbaths, a rushing down at the end of the prayer, as if glad to get out of God's presence." So many believing and so many enquiring souls used to attend, and so few of the worldlings, that you seemed to breathe the atmosphere of heaven.

But it was his Sabbath-day's services that brought multitudes together, and were soon felt throughout the town. He was ever so ready to assist his brethren, so much engaged in every good work, and latterly so often interrupted by inquiries, that it might be thought he had no time for careful preparation, and might be excused for the absence of it. But, in truth, he never preached without careful attention bestowed on his subject. He might, indeed, have little time— often the hours of a Saturday was all the time he could obtain—but his daily study of the Scriptures stored his mind, and formed a continual preparation. Much of his Sabbath

[1] The first text he gave to be thus hidden in the heart was Isaiah xxxiv. 15—"Until the Spirit be poured out from on high."

76

services was a drawing out of what he had carried in during busy days of the week.

His voice was remarkably clear—his manner attractive by its mild dignity. His form itself drew the eye.[1] He spoke from the pulpit as one earnestly occupied with the souls before him. He made them feel sympathy with what he spoke, for his own eye and heart were on them. He was, at the same time, able to bring out illustrations at once simple and felicitous, often with poetic skill and elegance. He wished to use Saxon words, for the sake of being understood by the most illiterate in his audience. And while his style was singularly clear, this clearness itself was so much the consequence of his being able thoroughly to analyse and explain his subject, that all his hearers alike reaped the benefit.

He went about his public work with awful reverence. So evident was this, that I remember a countryman in my parish observed to me—"Before he opened his lips, as he came along the passage, there was something about him that sorely affected me." In the vestry there was never any idle conversation; all was preparation of heart in approaching God; and a short prayer preceded his entering the pulpit. Surely in going forth to speak for God, a man may well be overawed! Surely in putting forth his hand to sow the seed of the kingdom, a man may even tremble! And surely we should aim at nothing less than to pour forth the truth upon our people through the channel of our own living and deeply affected souls.

After announcing the subject of his discourse, he used generally to show the position it occupied in the context, and then proceed to bring out the doctrines of the text in the manner of our old divines. This done, he divided his subject; and herein he was eminently skilful. "The heads of his sermons," said a friend, "were not the mile stones that tell you how near you are to your journey's end, but they were nails which fixed and fastened all he said. Divisions are often dry; but not so *his* divisions—they were so textual and so feeling, and they brought out the spirit of a passage so surprisingly."

It was his wish to arrive nearer at the primitive mode of

[1] "Gratior est pulchro veniens e corpore virtus."

77

expounding Scripture in his sermons. Hence when one asked him if he was never afraid of running short of sermons some day, he replied—"No; I am just an interpreter of Scripture in my sermons; and when the Bible runs dry, then I shall." And in the same spirit he carefully avoided the too common mode of accommodating texts—fastening a doctrine on the words, not drawing it from the obvious connection of the passage. He endeavoured at all times to *preach the mind of the Spirit in a passage;* for he feared that to do otherwise would be to grieve the Spirit who had written it. Interpretation was thus a solemn matter to him. And yet, adhering scrupulously to this sure principle, he felt himself in no way restrained from using, for every day's necessities, all parts of the Old Testament as much as the New. His manner was first to ascertain the primary sense and application, and so proceed to handle it for present use. Thus, on Isaiah xxvi. 16–19, he began—"This passage, I believe, refers *literally* to the conversion of God's ancient people." He regarded the *prophecies as history yet to be,* and drew lessons from them accordingly as he would have done from the past. Every spiritual gift being in the hands of Jesus, if he found Moses or Paul in the possession of precious things, he forthwith was led to follow them into the presence of that same Lord who gave them all their grace.

There is a wide difference between preaching *doctrine* and preaching *Christ.* Mr M'Cheyne preached all the doctrines of Scripture as understood by our Confession of Faith, dwelling upon ruin by the Fall, and recovery by the Mediator. "The things of the human heart, and the things of the Divine mind," were in substance his constant theme. From personal experience of deep temptation, he could lay open the secrets of the heart, so that he once said, "He supposed the reason why some of the worst sinners in Dundee had come to hear him was, because his heart exhibited so much likeness to theirs." Still it was not *doctrine* alone that he preached; it was *Christ,* from whom all doctrine shoots forth as rays from a centre. He sought to hang every vessel and flagon upon him. "It is strange," he wrote after preaching on Revelation i. 15—"It is strange how sweet and precious

78

it is to preach directly about Christ, compared with all other subjects of preaching." And he often expressed a dislike of the phrase, *"giving attention to religion,"* because it seemed to substitute doctrine, and a devout way of thinking, for *Christ himself*.

It is difficult to convey to those who never knew him a correct idea of the sweetness and holy unction of his preaching. Some of his sermons, printed from his own MSS. (although almost all are first copies), may convey a correct idea of his style and mode of preaching doctrine. But there are no notes that give any true idea of his affectionate appeals to the heart and searching applications. These he seldom wrote; they were poured forth at the moment when his heart filled with his subject; for his rule was to set before his hearers a body of truth first—and there always was a vast amount of Bible truth in his discourses—and then urge home the application. His exhortations flowed from his doctrine, and thus had both variety and power. He was systematic in this; for he observed—"Appeals to the careless, &c., come with power on the back of some massy truth. See how Paul does (Acts xiii. 40), 'Beware, *therefore*, lest,' &c., and (Hebrews ii. 1), '*Therefore*, we should,' &c."

He was sometimes a little unguarded in his statements, when his heart was deeply moved and his feelings stirred, and sometimes he was too long in his addresses; but this also arose from the fullness of his soul. "Another word," he thought, "may be blessed, though the last has made no impression."

Many will remember for ever the blessed Communion Sabbaths that were enjoyed in St Peter's. From the very first these Communion seasons were remarkably owned of God. The awe of his presence used to be upon his people, and the house filled with the odour of the ointment, when his name was poured forth. (Song i. 3.) But on common Sabbaths also many soon began to journey long distances to attend St Peter's—many from country parishes, who would return home with their hearts burning, as they talked of what they had heard that day.

Mr M'Cheyne knew the snare of popularity, and naturally was one that would have been fascinated by it; but the Lord kept him. He was sometimes extraordinarily helped in his preaching, but at other times, though not perceived by his hearers, his soul felt as if left to its own resources. The cry of Rowland Hill was constantly on his lips, "Master, help!" and often is it written at the close of his sermon. Much affliction, also, was a thorn in the flesh to him. He described himself as often "strong as a giant when in the Church, but like a willow-wand when all was over." But certainly, above all, his abiding sense of the Divine favour was his safeguard. He began his ministry in Dundee with this sunshine on his way. "As yet I have been kept not only in the light of his reconciled countenance, but very much under the guiding eye of our providing God. Indeed, as I remember good old Swartz used to say, 'I could not have imagined that he could have been so gracious to us.'" I believe that while he had some sorer conflicts, he had also far deeper joy after his return from Palestine than in the early part of his ministry, though from the very commencement of it, he enjoyed that sense of love of God which "keeps the heart and mind." (Philip. iv. 7.) This was the true secret of his holy walk, and of his calm humility. But for this, his ambition would have become the only principle of many an action; but now the sweeter peace of God constrained him, and the natural ambition of his spirit could be discerned only as suggesting to him the idea of making attempts which others would have declined.

What monotony there is in the ministry of many! Duty presses on the heels of duty in an endless circle. But it is not so when the Spirit is quickening both the pastor and his flock. Then there is all the variety of life. It was so here.

The Lord began to work by his means almost from the first day he came. There was ever one and another stricken, and going apart to weep alone.

The flocking of souls to his ministry, and the deep interest excited, drew the attention of many, and raised the wish in some quarters to have him as their pastor. He had not been many months engaged in his laborious work when he was solicited to remove to the parish of Skirling, near Biggar.

It was an offer that presented great advantages above his own field of labour as to worldly gain, and in respect of the prospect it held out of comparative ease and comfort; for the parish was small and the emolument great. But as it is required of a bishop, that he be "not greedy of filthy lucre"; nay, that he be "one who has no love of money" (ἀφιλάργυρος, 1 Tim. iii. 3) at all, so was it true that in him these qualifications eminently shone. His remarks in a letter to his father contain the honest expression of his feelings:—"I am set down among nearly 4000 people; 1100 people have taken seats in my church. I bring my message, such as it is, within the reach of that great company every Sabbath-day. I dare not leave this people. I dare not leave 3000 or 4000, for 300 people. Had this been offered me before, I would have seen it a direct intimation from God, and would heartily have embraced it. How I should have delighted to feed so precious a little flock—to watch over every family—to know every heart—'to allure to brighter worlds and lead the way!' But God has not so ordered it. He has set me down among the noisy mechanics and political weavers of this godless town. He will make the money sufficient. He that paid his taxes from a fish's mouth, will supply all my need." He had already expressed the hope, "Perhaps the Lord will make this wilderness of chimney-tops to be green and beautiful as the garden of the Lord, a field which the Lord hath blessed."

His health was delicate; and the harassing care and endless fatigue incident to his position, in a town like Dundee, seemed unsuitable to his spirit. This belief led to another attempt to remove him to a country sphere. In the summer of this same year (1837) he was strongly urged to preach as a candidate for the vacant parish of St Martin's, near Perth, and assured of the appointment if he would only come forward. But he declined again: "My Master has placed me here with his own hand; and I never will, directly or indirectly, seek to be removed."

There were circumstances in this latter case that made the call on him appear urgent in several points of view. In coming to a resolution, he mentions one interesting element in the decision, in a letter to me, dated August 8th. "I was much troubled about being asked to go to a neighbouring parish at present vacant, and made it a matter of prayer; and I mention it now because of the wonderful answer to prayer which I think I received from God. I prayed that in order to settle my own mind completely about staying, he would awaken some of my people. I agreed that that should be a sign he would wish me to stay. The next morning, I think, or at least the second morning, there came to me two young persons I had never seen before, in great distress. What brought this to my mind was, that they came to me again yesterday, and their distress is greatly increased. Indeed I never saw any people in such anguish about their soul. I cannot but regard this as a real answer to prayer. I have also several other persons in deep distress, and I feel that I am quite helpless in comforting them. I would fain be like Noah, who put out his hand and took in the weary dove; but God makes me stand by and feel that I am a child. Will God never cast the scenes of our labour near each other? We are in his hand; let him do as seemeth him good. Pray for me, for my people, for my own soul, that I be not a castaway."

Few godly pastors can be willing to change the scene of their labours, unless it be plain that the Cloudy Pillar is pointing them away. It is perilous for men to choose for themselves; and too often has it happened that the minister who, on slight grounds, moved away from his former watchtower, has had reason to mourn over the disappointment of his hopes in his larger and wider sphere. But while this is admitted, probably it may appear unwarrantable in Mr M'Cheyne to have prayed for a sign of the Lord's will. It is to be observed, however, that he decided the point of duty on other grounds, and it was only with the view of obtaining an additional confirmation by the occurrences of Providence, that he prayed in this manner, in submission to the will of the Lord. He never held it right to decide the path of duty by any such signs or tokens; he believed that the written word supplied sufficient data for guiding the believing soul; and such providential occurrences as happened in this case he regarded as important only so far as they might be

policy, in his view, could be more ruinous to true Christianity, or more fitted to blight vital godliness, than that of Moderatism. He wrote once to a friend in Ireland—"You don't know what Moderatism is. It is a plant that our Heavenly Father never planted, and I trust it is now to be rooted up." The great question of the Church's independence of the Civil Power in all matters spiritual, and the right of the Christian people to judge if the pastor appointed over them had the Shepherd's voice, he invariably held to be part of Scripture truth; which, therefore, must be preached and carried into practice, at all hazards. In like manner he rejoiced exceedingly in the settlements of faithful ministers. The appointments of Mr Baxter to Hilltown, Mr Lewis to St David's, and Mr Miller to Wallacetown at a later period, are all noticed by him with expressions of thankfulness and joy; and it occasioned the same feelings if he heard of the destitution of any parish in any part of the country supplied. He writes, September 20, 1838. "Present at A. B.'s ordination at Collace with great joy. Blessed be God for the gift of this pastor. Give testimony to the word of thy grace."

Busy at home, he nevertheless always had a keenly evangelistic spirit. He might have written much, and have gained a name by his writings; but he laid everything aside when put in comparison with preaching the everlasting gospel. He scarcely ever refused an invitation to preach on a week-day; and travelling from place to place did not interrupt his fellowship with God. His occasional visits during these years were much blessed. At Blairgowrie and Collace his visits were longed for as times of special refreshment; nor was it less so at Kirriemuir, when he visited Mr Cormick, or at Abernyte in the days when Mr Hamilton (now of Regent Square, London) and afterwards Mr Manson, were labouring in that vineyard. It would be difficult even to enumerate the places which he watered at Communion seasons; and in some of these it was testified of him, that not the words he spoke, but the *holy manner* in which he spoke, was the chief means of arresting souls.

Occasionally two or three of us, whose lot was cast within convenient distance, and whose souls panted for the same water-brooks, used to meet together to spend a whole day in confession of ministerial and personal sins, with prayer for grace, guiding ourselves by the reading of the Word. At such times we used to meet in the evening with the flock of the pastor in whose house the meeting had been held through the day, and there unitedly pray for the Holy Spirit being poured down upon the people. The first time we held such a meeting, there were tokens of blessing observed by several of us; and the week after, he wrote—"Has there been any fruit of the happy day we spent with you? I thought I saw some the Sabbath after, here. In due season we shall reap if we faint not; only be thou strong, and of a good courage." The incident that encouraged him is recorded in his diary. An elderly person came to tell him how the river of joy and peace in believing had that Sabbath most singularly flowed through her soul, so that she blessed God that she ever came to St Peter's. He adds, "N.B.—This seems a fruit of our prayer-meeting, begun last Wednesday at Collace—one drop of the shower."

It should have been remarked ere now, that during all his ministry he was careful to use not only the direct means appointed for the conversion of souls, but those also that appear more indirect, such as the key of discipline. In regard to the Lord's Supper, his little tract explains his views. He believed that to keep back those whose profession was a credible profession, even while the pastor might have strong doubts as to their fitness in his own mind, was not the rule laid down for us in the New Testament. At the same time, he as steadily maintained that no unconverted person *ought to come* to the Lord's Table; and on this point "they should judge themselves if they would not be judged."

When communicants came to be admitted for the first time, or when parents that had been communicants before came for baptism to their children, it was his custom to ask them solemnly if their souls were saved. His dealing was blessed to the conversion of not a few young persons who were coming carelessly forward to the communion; and himself records the blessing that attended his faithful dealing with a parent coming to speak with him about the baptism of his child. The man said that he had been taking thought, and believed himself in the right way—that he felt his disposition better, for he could forgive injuries. Mr M'Cheyne showed him that nevertheless he was ignorant of God's righteousness. The man laid it to heart; and when Mr M'Cheyne said that he thought it would be better to defer the baptism, at once offered to come again and speak on the matter. On a subsequent visit, he seemed really to have seen his error, and to have cast away his own righteousness. When his child was baptised, it was joy to the pastor's heart to have the good hope that the man had received salvation.

In connection with the superstitious feeling of the most depraved as to baptism, he related an affecting occurrence. A careless parent one evening entered his house, and asked him to come with him to baptize a dying child. He knew that neither this man nor his wife ever entered the door of a church; but he rose and went with him to the miserable dwelling. There an infant lay, apparently dying; and many of the female neighbours, equally depraved with the parents, stood round. He came forward to where the child was, and spoke to the parents of their ungodly state and fearful guilt before God, and concluded by showing them that, in such circumstances, he would consider it sinful in him to administer baptism to their infant. They said, "He might at least do it for the sake of the poor child." He told them that it was not baptism that saved a soul, and that out of true concern for themselves he must not do as they wished. The friends around the bed then joined the parents in upbraiding him as having no pity on the poor infant's soul! He stood among them still, and showed them that it was they who had been thus cruel to their child; and then lifted up his voice in solemn warning, and left the house amid their ignorant reproaches.

Nor did he make light of the Kirk-session's power to rebuke and deal with an offender. Once from the pulpit, at an ordination of elders, he gave the following testimony upon this head:—"When I first entered upon the work of the ministry among you, I was exceedingly ignorant of the vast importance of church discipline. I thought that my great and almost only work was to pray and preach. I saw your souls to be so precious, and the time so short, that I devoted all my time, and care, and strength, to labour in word and doctrine. When cases of discipline were brought before me and the elders, I regarded them with something like abhorrence. It was a duty I shrank from; and I may truly say it nearly drove me from the work of the ministry among you altogether. But it pleased God, who teaches his servants in another way than man teaches, to bless some of the cases of discipline to the manifest and undeniable conversion of the souls of those under our care; and from that hour a new light broke in upon my mind, and I saw that if preaching be an ordinance of Christ, so is church discipline. I now feel very deeply persuaded that both are of God—that two keys are committed to us by Christ, the one the key of doctrine, by means of which we unlock the treasures of the Bible, the other the key of discipline, by which we open or shut the way to the sealing ordinances of the faith. Both are Christ's gift, and neither is to be resigned without sin."

There was still another means of enforcing what he preached, in the use of which he has excelled all his brethren, namely, the holy consistency of his daily walk. Aware that one idle word, one needless contention, one covetous act, may destroy in our people the effect of many a solemn expostulation and earnest warning, he was peculiarly circumspect in his every-day walk. He wished to be always in the presence of God. If he travelled, he laboured to enjoy God by the way, as well as to do good to others by dropping a word in season. In riding or walking, he seized opportunities of giving a useful tract; and, on principle, he preferred giving it to the person directly, rather than casting it on the road. The former way, he said, was more open—there was no stealth in it—and we ought to be as clear as crystal in speaking or acting for Jesus. In writing a note, however short, he sought to season it with salt. If he passed a night in a strange place, he tried to bear the place specially on his soul at the mercy-seat; and if compelled to take some rest from his too exhausting toils, his recreations were little else than a change of occupation, from one mode of glorifying

God to another.[1] His beautiful hymn, *"I am a debtor,"* was written in May 1837 at a leisure hour.

Whatever be said in the pulpit, men will not much regard, though they may feel it at the time, if the minister does not say the same in private, with equal earnestness, in speaking with his people face to face; and it must be in our moments of most familiar intercourse with them, that we are thus to put the seal to all we say in public. Familiar moments are the times when the things that are most closely twined round the heart are brought out to view; and shall we forbear, by tacit consent, to introduce the Lord that bought us into such happy hours? We must not only speak faithfully to our people in our sermons, but live faithfully for them too. Perhaps it may be found, that the reason why many, who preach the gospel fully and in all earnestness, are not owned of God in the conversion of souls, is to be found in their defective exhibition of grace in these easy moments of life. "Them that honour me, I will honour;" 1 Samuel ii. 30. It was noticed long ago that men will give you leave to *preach against* their sins as much as you will, if so be you will but be easy with them when you have done, and talk as they do, and live as they live. How much otherwise it was with Mr M'Cheyne, all who knew him are witnesses!

His visits to friends were times when he sought to do good to their souls; and never was he satisfied unless he could guide the conversation to bear upon the things of eternity. When he could not do so, he generally remained silent. And yet his demeanour was easy and pleasant to all, exhibiting at once meekness of faith, and delicacy of feeling. There was in his character a high refinement that came out in poetry and true politeness; and there was something in his graces that reminded one of his own remark, when explaining *"the*

---

[1] Baxter's words are not less than the truth. "Recreation to a minister must be as whetting is with the mower, that is, only to be used so far as is necessary for his work. May a physician in the plague-time take any more relaxation or recreation than is necessary for his life, when so many are expecting his help in a case of life and death?" "Will you stand by and see sinners gasping under the pangs of death, and say, God doth not require me to make myself a drudge to save them? Is this the voice of ministerial or Christian compassion, or rather of *sensual laziness and diabolical cruelty*?"—*Reformed Pastor* vi. 6.

spices" of Song iv. 16, when he said, that "some believers were a garden that had fruit trees, and so were useful; but we ought also to have *spices* and so be attractive." Wishing to convey his grateful feelings to a fellow labourer in Dundee, he sent him a Hebrew Bible, with these few lines prefixed :—

"Anoint mine eyes,
  O holy Dove!
That I may prize
  This book of love.

Unstop mine ear,
  Made deaf by sin,
That I may hear
  Thy voice within.

Break my hard heart,
  Jesus, my Lord,
In the inmost part
  Hide thy sweet word.

It was on a similar occasion, in 1838, that he wrote the lines, "*Thy word is a lamp unto my feet.*" At another time, sitting under a shady tree, and casting his eye on the hospitable dwelling in which he found a pleasant retreat, his grateful feelings flowed out to his kind friend in the lines that follow :—

"PEACE TO THIS HOUSE"

Long may peace within this dwelling
  Have its resting place;
Angel shields all harm repelling—
  God, their God of grace.

May the dove-like Spirit guide them
  To the upright land !
May the Saviour-Shepherd feed them
  From his gentle hand !

Never was there one more beloved as a friend, and seldom any whose death could cause so many to feel as if no other friend could ever occupy his room. Some, too, can say that so much did they learn from his holy walk, "that it is probable a day never passes wherein they have not some advantage from his friendship." [1]

I find written on the leaf of one of his note-books, a short

[1] Ἐγὼ μὲν δὴ κατανοῶν τοῦ ἀνδρὸς τήν τε σοφίαν καὶ τὴν γενναιότητα, οὔτε μὴ μεμνῆσθαι δύναμαι αὐτοῦ,οὔτε μεμνημένος μὴ οὐκ ἐπαινεῖν. Εἰ δέ τις τῶν ἀρετῆς ἐφιεμένων ὠφελιμωτέρῳ τινὶ Σωκράτους συνεγένετο, ἐκεῖνον ἐγὼ τὸν ἄνδρα ἀξιομακαριστότατον νομίζω.

memorandum : "*Rules worth remembering.*—When visiting in a family, whether ministerially or otherwise, speak particularly to *the strangers* about eternal things. Perhaps God has brought you together just to save that soul." And then he refers to some instances which occurred to himself, in which God seemed to honour a word spoken in this incidental way.

In this spirit, he was enabled for nearly three years to give his strength to his Master's service. Sickness sometimes laid him aside, and taught him what he had to suffer; but he rose from it to go forth again to his joyful labours. Often, after a toilsome day, there were inquirers waiting for him, so that he had to begin work afresh in a new form. But this was his delight; it was a kind of interruption which he allowed even on a Saturday, in the midst of his studies. He was led to resolve not to postpone any inquirers till a future time, by finding that having done so on one occasion at a pressing moment, the individuals never returned; and so alive was he to the responsibilities of his office, that he ever after feared to lose such an opportunity of speaking with souls at a time when they were aroused to concern. Busy one evening with some extra-parochial work, he was asked if any person should be admitted to see him that night. "Surely —what do we live for?" was his immediate reply. It was his manner, too, on a Saturday afternoon, to visit one or two of his sick who seemed near the point of death, with the view of being thus stirred up to a more direct application of the truth to his flock on the morrow, as dying men on the edge of eternity.

We have already observed that in his doctrine there was nothing that differed from the views of truth laid down in the standards of our Church. He saw no inconsistency in preaching an electing God, who "calleth whom he will," and a salvation free to "whosoever will;" nor in declaring the absolute sovereignty of God, and yet the unimpaired responsibility of man. He preached Christ as a gift laid down by the Father for every sinner freely to take. In the beginning of his ministry, as he preached the fullness of the glad tidings, and urged on his people that there was enough in the glad tidings to bring direct and immediate assurance to every one who really believed them, some of his flock were startled. For he ever preached, that, while it is true that there are believers, like Heman or Asaph, who do not enjoy full assurance of the love of God, yet certainly no true believer should remain satisfied in the absence of this blessed peace. Not a few had hitherto been accustomed to take for granted that they might be Christians, though they knew of no change; and had never thought of enjoying the knowledge of the love of God as their present portion. They heard that others, who were reckoned believers, had doubts; so they had come to consider fears and doubts as the very marks of a believing soul. The consequence had been, that, in past days, many concluded themselves to be Christians, because they seemed to be in the very state of mind of which those who were reputed to be believers spoke, viz., doubt and alarm. Alas! in *their* case there could be nothing else, for they had only a name to live.

Someone wrote to him, putting several questions concerning conversion, assurance, and faith, which had been stirred up by his ministry. The import of the questions may be gathered from his reply, which was as follows:—

"1. *I doubt if there are many saints who live and die without a comfortable sense of forgiveness, and acceptance with God.* The saints of whom the Bible speaks seem to have enjoyed it richly both in life and death. See the murderers of our Lord, Acts ii. 41; the Ethiopian, Acts viii. 39; the jailor, Acts xvi. 35. David also felt it, sinful man though he was, Romans iv. 6. Paul also prayed that the Romans might have it, Romans xv. 13. I fear this objection is generally made by those who are living in sin, and do not wish to know the dangerous road they are on.

"2. *A sense of forgiveness does not proceed from marks seen in yourself, but from a discovery of the beauty, worth, and freeness of Christ;* Psa. xxxiv. 5. We look *out* for peace not *in*. At the same time there is also an assurance rising from what we see in ourselves: the seal of the Spirit, love to the brethren, &c., are the chief marks.

"3. *Feeling a body of sin is a mark that we are like Paul, and that we are Christ's;* Rom. vii; Gal. v. 17. Paul was

92

cheerful with a body of sin; and so ought we to be. So was David, and all the saints.

"4. *I do not think there is any difference between those converted within these few years, and those who were Christians before.* Many of those converted since I came are, I fear, very unholy. I fear this more than anything. I fear there is too much talk and too little reality. Still there are many good figs—many of whom I am persuaded better things, and things that accompany salvation. The answer to your question I fear is this, that many used to be taken for Christians before, who had only a name to live, and were dead. I think there is more discrimination now. But take care and be not proud, for that goes before a fall. Take care of censorious judging of others, as if all must be converted in the same way.

"God moves in a mysterious way. He hath mercy on whom he will have mercy. To him alone be glory."

He thus stated his views on another occasion: Referring to Song vi. 3, "My Beloved is mine," following "My Beloved is gone down into his garden," he said, "This is the faith of assurance—a complete, unhesitating embracing of Christ as my righteousness and my strength and my all. A common mistake is that this clear conviction that Christ is mine, is an attainment far on in the divine life, and that it springs from evidences seen in my heart. When I see myself a new creature, Christ on the throne in my heart, love to the brethren, &c., it is often thought that I may begin then to say 'My Beloved is mine.' How different this passage! The moment Jesus comes down into the garden to the beds of spices—the moment he reveals himself, the soul cries out, 'My Beloved is mine!' So saith Thomas: John xx. 27, 28. The moment Jesus came in and revealed his wounds, Thomas cried out, 'My Lord and my God.' He did not look to see if he was believing, or if the graces of love and humility were reigning; but all he saw and thought of was Jesus and him crucified and risen." At a subsequent period, when preaching on Matt. xi. 28, "Come unto me," he said, "I suppose it is almost impossible to explain what it is to come to Jesus, it is so simple. If you ask a sick person who had been

93

healed, what it was to come and be healed, he could hardly tell you. As far as the Lord has given me light in this matter, and looking at what my own heart does in like circumstances, I do not feel that there is anything more in coming to Jesus, than just believing what God says about his Son to be true. I believe that many people keep themselves in darkness by expecting something more than this. Some of you will ask, 'Is there no *appropriating* of Christ? no *putting out the hand of faith*? no touching the hem of his garment?' I quite grant, beloved, there is such a thing, but I do think it is inseparable from believing the record. If the Lord persuades you of the glory and power of Immanuel, I feel persuaded that you cannot but choose him. It is like opening the shutters of a dark room; the sun that moment shines in. So, the eye that is opened to the testimony of God, receives Christ that moment.'

In the case of a faithful ministry, success is the rule; want of it the exception. For it is written, "In doing this thou shalt both save thyself and them that hear thee;" 1 Tim. iv. 16. Mr M'Cheyne expected it, and the Lord exceeded all his hopes.

It was not yet common for persons in anxiety to go to their pastor for advice; but soon it became an almost weekly occurrence. While it was yet rare, two of his young people wrote a joint note, asking liberty to come and speak with him, "For we are anxious about our souls." Among those who came, there were those who had striven against the truth—persons, who used to run out of hearing when the Bible was read—throw down a tract if the name of God was in it—go quickly to sleep after a Sabbath's pleasure in order to drown the fear of dropping into hell. There were many whose whole previous life had been but a threadbare profession. There were some open sinners, too. In short, the Lord glorified himself by the variety of those whom his grace subdued, and the variety of means by which his grace reached its object.

One could tell him that the reading of the chapter in the church with a few remarks, had been the time of her awakening. Another had been struck to the heart by some expression he used in his first prayer before sermon one Sabbath morning. But most were arrested in the preaching of the Word. An interesting case was that of one who was aroused to concern during his sermon on "*Unto whom coming as unto a living stone.*" As he spoke of the Father taking the gem out of his bosom, and laying it down for a foundation-stone, she felt in her soul, "I know nothing of this precious stone; I am surely not converted." This led her to come and speak with him. She was not under deep conviction; but before going away he said, "You are a poor, vile worm; it is a wonder the earth does not open and swallow you up." These words were blessed to produce a very awful sense of sin. She came a second time with the arrows of the Almighty drinking up her spirit. For three months she remained in this state, till having once more come to him for counsel, the living voice of Jesus gave life to her soul while he was speaking of Christ's words—"If thou knewest the gift of God," &c., and she went away rejoicing. Some awakened souls told him that since they were brought under concern, very many sermons, which they had heard from him before, and completely forgotten, had been brought back to mind. He used to remark that this might show what the Resurrection day would awaken in the souls of gospel hearers.

In dealing with souls he used to speak very plainly. One came to him who assented to his statements of the gospel, and yet refused to be comforted, always looking upon *coming to Christ* as something in addition to really believing the record God has given of his Son. He took John iii. 16, 17— "For God so loved the world that," &c. The woman said that "God did not care for her." Upon this he at once convicted her of making God a liar; and, as she went away in deep distress, his prayer was—"Lord, give her light."

To another person, who spoke of having times of great joy, he shewed that these were times for worshipping God in the spirit. "You would come to a king when you were full dressed; so come to God, and abide in his presence as long as you can."

Sometimes he would send away souls, of whom he entertained good hope, with a text suited to their state. "If ye live after the flesh, ye shall die; but if ye, through the Spirit, do mortify the deeds of the body, ye shall live." Or he would say, "I hear of you that God has opened your heart; but remember not to trust to man's opinion. Remember an all-seeing Christ will be the judge at the great day." To another he said, "I have long hoped you were really under the wings of the Saviour: if it be so, abide there; do not be like Demas."

To a prayer-meeting, consisting of a few young men that had been awakened to flee from wrath, he gave this advice, "Guard against all ambition to excel one another in expression. Remember the most spiritual prayer is a 'groan which cannot be uttered,' Rom. viii. 26; or a cry of 'Abba, Father,' Gal. iv. 6."

There is very little recorded in his diary during these years; but what does exist will be read with deepest interest.

"March 28. 1838, Thursday.—I think of making this more a journal of my people, and the success, or otherwise, of my ministry. The first success among my people was at the time of my first sacrament: then it appeared. My first sermon, on Isaiah lxi. 1, was blessed to —— and some others. That on Ezek. xxii. 14, 'Can thine heart endure,' &c., was blessed to awaken M. L. That on Song v. 2, 'Open to me,' &c., the Sabbath after the Sacrament, was blessed to another. These were happy days. M. D. was awakened by coming to the communicants' class. Another by the action sermon. At the words, 'I know thee, Judas,' she trembled, and would have risen from the table. These were glad days when one and another were awakened. The people looked very stirred and anxious, every day coming to hear the words of eternal life—some inquiring in private every week. Now there is little of this. About fifteen cases came to my knowledge the first Sacrament, and two awakened who seem to have gone back. About eleven last Sacrament—four of these young men. Several Christians seemed quickened to greater joy, and greater love one to another. Now it appears to me there is much falling off: few seem awakened—few weep as they used to do.

"April 1—Sacrament-day.—Sweet season we have had.

Never was more straitened and unfurnished in myself, and yet much helped. Kept in perfect peace, my mind being stayed on Thee. Preached on 'My God, my God, &c.; Psalm xxii. 1. Not fully prepared, yet found some peace in it. Fenced the tables from Christ's eyes of flame.' Little helped in serving the tables. Much peace in communion. Happy to be one with Christ! *I*, a vile worm; *He*, the Lord my righteousness. Mr Cumming of Dumbarney served some tables; Mr Somerville of Anderston served three, and preached in the evening on, 'Thou art all fair, my love.' Very full and refreshing. All sweet sweet services. Come, thou north wind, and blow, thou south, upon this garden! May this time be greatly blessed! It is my third communion; it may be my last. My Lord may come, or I may be sitting at another table soon. Moody, Candlish, and Mellis, were a good preparation for this day; and the sweet word from Cumming yesterday, 'When the poor and needy seek water,' &c. Lord, grant some awakening this day—to some bringing peace—comfort to mourners—fullness to believers—an advance in holiness in me and my children! 3 John iv. Lord, wean me from my sins, from my cares, and from this passing world. May Christ be all in all to me.

"Admitted about twenty-five young communicants; kept two back, and one or two stayed back. Some of them evidently brought to Christ. May the Lord be their God, their comforter, their all! May the morrow bring still richer things to us, that we may say as of to-night, 'Thou hast kept the good wine until now.'"

Toward the close of this same year, some of his notices are as follows:—

"October 7—Evening.—In the Gaelic Chapel, on 'I know that my Redeemer liveth,' with more seeming power on the people than for a while. I never remember of compelling souls to come into Christ so much as in that discourse."

"Oct. 8.—A person of the name of —— came; I hope really awakened by last night's work; rather, by *thee*. I do not know, however, whether *grace* is begun or not."

"Oct. 14.—Preached on 'Forgiving injuries.' Afternoon—on the Second Coming: 'Let your loins be girded about,'

&c. Felt its power myself more than ever before, how the sudden coming of the Saviour constrains to a holy walk, separate from sin. Evening—Preached it over in the Ferry."

"Oct. 21.—Met young communicants in the evening. Good hope of all but one."

"Oct. 22.—A Jew preached in my church, Mr Frey, to a crowded house. Felt much moved in hearing an Israelite after the flesh."

"Oct. 23.—Preached to sailors aboard the 'Dr Carey,' in the Docks. About 200, very attentive and impressed-like. On 'I know that my Redeemer liveth.' May the seed sown on the waters be found after many days."

November 1—Fast-day.—Afternoon—Mr C. on 'The Thief on the Cross.' A most awakening and engaging sermon, enough to make sinners fly like a cloud, and as doves to their windows. The offers of Christ were let down very low, so that those low of stature may take hold."

"Nov. 5.—Mr —— died this morning at seven o'clock. O that I may take warning, lest, after preaching to others, I myself be a castaway. Love of popularity is said to have been his besetting sin."

"December 2.—Errol communion. Heard Mr Grierson preach on Christ's entry into Jerusalem. Served two tables. Evening—Preached to a large congregation, on 'Unto you, O men, I call,' &c. The free invitation of the Saviour. May some find him this day!"

In addition to the other blessings which the Lord sent by his means to the place where he laboured, it was obvious to all that the tone of Christians was raised, as much by his holy walk, as by his heavenly ministry. Yet, during these pleasant days, he had much reproach to bear. He was the object of supercilious contempt to formal, cold-hearted ministers, and of bitter hatred to many of the ungodly. At this day, there are both ministers and professing Christians of whom Jesus would say, "The world cannot hate you," (John vii. 7), for the world cannot hate itself; but it was not so with Mr M'Cheyne. Very deep was the enmity borne to him by some—all the deeper, because the only cause of it was his likeness to his Master. But nothing turned him aside. He was full of ardour, yet ever gentle, and meek and generous; full of zeal, yet never ruffled by his zeal; and not only his strength of "first love" (Rev. ii. 4.), but even its warm glow, seemed in him to suffer no decay.

Thus he spent the first years of his ministry in Dundee. The town began to feel that they had a peculiar man of God in the midst of them; for he lived as a true son of Levi. "My covenant was with him of life and peace, and I gave them to him for the fear wherewith he feared me, and was afraid before my name. The law of truth was in his mouth, and iniquity was not found in his lips; he walked with me in peace and equity, and did turn many away from iniquity;" Mal. ii. 5, 6.

CHAPTER IV

HIS MISSION TO PALESTINE
AND THE JEWS

"Here am I; send me."—ISAIAH vi. 8.

THOUGH engaged night and day with his flock in St Peter's, Mr M'Cheyne ever cherished a missionary spirit. "This place hardens me for a foreign land," was his remark on one occasion. This spirit he sought to kindle yet more by reading missionary intelligence for his own use, and often to his people at his weekly prayer-meeting. The necessities both of his own parish, and of the world at large, lay heavy on his soul; and when an opportunity of evangelizing occurred, there was none in Scotland more ready to embrace it. He seemed one who stood with his loins girt—"Here am I; send me."

Another motive to incessant activity, was the decided impression on his mind that his career would be short. From the very first days of his ministry he had a strong feeling of this nature; and his friends remember how his letters used to be sealed with this seal, *"The night cometh."* At a time when he was apparently in his usual health, we were talking together on the subject of the Premillennial Advent. We had begun to speak of the practical influence which the belief of that doctrine might have. At length he said that he saw no force in the arguments generally urged against it, though he had difficulties of his own in regard to it. And, perhaps (he added), it is well for you, who enjoy constant health, to be so firmly persuaded that Christ is thus to come; but my sickly frame makes me feel every day that my time may be very short.

He was, therefore, in some measure prepared, when, in the midst of his laborious duties, he was compelled to stand still and see what the Lord would do.

In the close of 1838, some symptoms appeared that alarmed his friends. His constitution, never robust, began to feel the effects of unremitting labour; for, occasionally, he would spend six hours in visiting, and then, the same evening, preach in some room to all the families whom he had that day visited. Very generally, too, on Sabbath, after preaching twice to his own flock, he was engaged in ministering somewhere else in the evening. But now, after any great exertion, he was attacked by violent palpitation of heart. It soon increased, affecting him in his hours of study; and, at last, it became almost constant. Upon this, his medical advisers insisted on a total cessation of his public work; for though, as yet, there was no organic change on his lungs, there was every reason to apprehend that that might be the result. Accordingly, with deep regret, he left Dundee to seek rest and change of occupation, hoping it would be only for a week or two.

A few days after leaving Dundee, he writes from Edinburgh, in reply to the anxious inquiries of his friend Mr Grierson, "The beating of the heart is not now so constant as it was before. The pitcher draws more quietly at the cistern; so that, by the kind providence of our Heavenly Father, I may be spared a little longer before the silver cord be loosed, and the golden bowl be broken."

It was found that his complaints were such as would be likely to give way under careful treatment, and a temporary cessation from all exertion. Under his father's roof, therefore, in Edinburgh, he resigned himself to the will of his Father in heaven. But deeply did he feel the trial of being laid aside from his loved employment, though he learnt of Him who was meek and lowly, to make the burden light in his own way, by saying, "Even so, Father, for so it seemeth good in thy sight." He wrote to Mr Grierson again, January 5, 1839, "I hope this affliction will be blessed to me. I always feel much need of God's afflicting hand. In the whirl of active labour there is so little time for watching, and for bewailing, and seeking grace, to oppose the sins of our ministry, that I always feel it a blessed thing when the Saviour takes me aside from the crowd, as he took the blind man out of the town, and removes the veil, and clears away obscuring mists; and by his Word and Spirit leads to deeper peace and a holier walk. Ah! there is nothing like a calm look into the eternal world to teach us the emptiness of human praise, the sinfulness of self-seeking and vain glory—to teach us the preciousness of Christ, who is called 'The Tried Stone.' I have been able to be twice at College to hear a lecture from Dr Chalmers. I have also been privileged to smooth down the dying pillow of an old school-companion, leading him to a fuller joy and peace in believing. A poor heavy-laden soul, too, from Larbert, I have had the joy of leading toward the Saviour. So that even when absent from my work, and when exiled, as it were, God allows me to do some little things for his name."

He was led to look more carefully into this trying dispensation, and began to anticipate blessed results from it to his flock. He was well aware how easily the flock begin to idolize the shepherd, and how prone the shepherd is to feel somewhat pleased with this sinful partiality of his people, and to be uplifted by his success. "I sometimes think," is his remark in a letter, dated January 18, "that a great blessing may come to my people in my absence. Often God does not bless us when we are in the midst of our labours, lest we shall say, 'My hand and my eloquence have done it.' He removes us into silence, and then pours 'down a blessing so that there is no room to receive it;' so that all that see it cry out,' 'It is the Lord!' This was the way in the South Sea Islands. May it really be so with my dear people!" Nor did he err in this view of the dispensation. All these ends, and more also, were to be accomplished by it.

An anticipation like that which is expressed in this and other letters, especially in his Pastoral Letter of March 20, may justly be regarded as a proof from experience that the Lord teaches his people to expect and pray for what he means soon to work. And here the Lord accomplished his designs in the kindest of all ways; for he removed his servant for a season from the flock to which he had been so blessed, lest even his own children should begin to glory in man; but yet he took that servant to another sphere of labour in the meantime; and then, when the blessing was safely bestowed, brought him back to rejoice over it.

He was still hoping for, and submissively asking from the Lord, speedy restoration to his people in Dundee, and occasionally sending to them an epistle that breathed the true pastor's soul; when one day, as he was walking with Dr Candlish, conversing on the Mission to Israel which had lately been resolved on, an idea seemed suddenly suggested to Dr Candlish. He asked Mr M'Cheyne what he would think of "being useful to the Jewish cause, during his cessation from labour, by going abroad to make personal inquiries into the state of Israel?" The idea, thus suddenly suggested, led to all the after results of the Mission of Inquiry. Mr M'Cheyne found himself all at once called to carry salvation to the Jew, as he had hitherto done to the Gentile, and his soul was filled with joy and wonder. His medical friends highly approved of the proposal, as being likely to conduce very much to the removal of his complaints—the calm, steady excitement of such a journey being likely to restore the tone of his whole constitution.

Dr Black of Aberdeen readily consented to use his remarkable talents as a scholar in this cause; and Dr Keith intimated his expectation of soon joining the deputation. I also had been chosen to go forth on this mission of love to Israel; but some difficulties stood in the way of my leaving my charge at Collace. In these circumstances, Mr M'Cheyne wrote to me, March 12, from Edinburgh.

"My dear A.—I have received so many tokens for good from God in this matter, that it were a shame indeed if I did not trust him to perfect all which concerns me. I am glad you have determined to trust all in the hands of Israel's God. I am quite ready to go this week, or next week, but am deeply anxious to be sure that you are sent with me. You know, dear A., I could not labour in this cause, nor enjoy it, if you were not to be with me in it. Would you be ready to give your Jewish lecture on the evening of Sabbath week? * * * And now, pray for us, that we may be sent of God; and, weak as we are, that we may be made Boanerges—that we may be blessed to win some souls, and to stir up Christians to love Zion. Much interest is already excited, and I do look for a blessing. Speak to your people as on the brink of eternity. * * * As to books, I am quite at a loss. My Hebrew Bible, Greek Testament, &c., and perhaps Bridge's *Christian Ministry* for general purposes—I mean, for keeping us in mind of our ministerial work. I do hope we shall go forth in the Spirit; and though straitened in language, may we not be blessed, as Brainerd was, through an interpreter? May we not be blessed also to save some English, and to stir up missionaries? My health is only tolerable; I would be better if we were once away. I am often so troubled, as to be made willing to go or stay, to die or to live. Yet it is encouraging to be used in the Lord's service again, and in so interesting a manner. What if we should see the heavenly Jerusalem before the earthly? I am taking drawing materials, that I may carry away remembrances of the Mount of Olives, Tabor, and the Sea of Galilee."

The interest that this proposed journey excited in Scotland was very great. Nor was it merely the somewhat romantic interest attached to the land where the Lord had done most of his mighty works; there were also in it the deeper feelings of a Scriptural persuasion that Israel was still "beloved for the fathers' sake." For some time previous, Jerusalem had come into mind, and many godly pastors were standing as watchmen over its ruined walls (Isa. lxii. 6), stirring up the Lord's remembrancers. Mr M'Cheyne had been one of these. His views of the importance of the Jews in the eye of God, and, therefore, of their importance as a sphere of missionary labour, were very clear and decided. He agreed in the expectation expressed in one of the Course of Lectures delivered before the deputation set out, that we might anticipate an *outpouring of the Spirit when our Church should stretch out its hands to the Jew as well as to the Gentile.* In one letter, he says, "To seek the lost sheep of the house of Israel is an object very near to my heart, as my people know it has ever been. Such an enterprise may probably draw down unspeakable blessings on the Church of Scotland, according to the promise, 'they shall prosper who love thee'." In another, "I now see plainly that all our views about the Jews being the chief object of missionary exertion are plain and sober truths, according to the Scripture." Again, "I feel convinced that if we pray that the world may be converted in God's way, we will seek the good of the Jews, and the more we do so, the happier we will be in our own soul. You should always keep up a knowledge of the prophecies regarding Israel." In his preaching he not unfrequently said on this subject, "We should be like God in his peculiar affections; and the whole Bible shows that God has ever had, and still has, a peculiar love to the Jews."

The news of his proposed absence alarmed his flock at Dundee. They manifested their care for him more than ever; and not a few wrote expostulatory letters. To one of these well-meant remonstrances, he replied, "I rejoice exceedingly in the interest you take in me, not so much for my own sake as that I hope it is a sign you know and love the Lord Jesus. Unless God had himself shut up the door of return to my people, and opened this new door to me, I never could have consented to go. I am not at all unwilling to spend and be spent in God's service, though I have often found that the more abundantly I love you, the less I am loved. But God has very plainly shewn me that I may perform a deeply important work for his ancient people, and at the same time be in the best way of seeking a return of health."—"A minister will make a poor saviour in the day of wrath. It is not knowing a minister, or loving one, or hearing one, or having a name to live that will save. You need to have your hand on the head of the Lamb for yourselves; Lev. i. 4. You need to have your eye on the brazen serpent for yourselves; John iii. 14, 15. I fear I will need to be a swift witness against many of my people in the day of the Lord, that they looked to me, and not to Christ, when I preached to them. I always feared that some of you loved to hear the Word, who do not love to do it. I always feared there were many of you who loved the Sabbath meetings, and the class, and the Thursday evenings, who yet were not careful to walk with God, to be meek, chaste, holy, loving, harmless, Christ-like, God-like. Now, God wants you to think, that the only end of a gospel ministry is, that you may be holy. Believe me, God himself could not make you happy, except you be holy."

At this crisis in his people's history he sought from the Lord one to supply his place—one who would feed the flock and gather in wanderers during their own pastor's absence. The Lord granted him his desire by sending Mr William C. Burns, son of the minister of Kilsyth. In a letter to him, dated March 12th, the following remarkable words occur:— "You are given in answer to prayer, and these gifts are, I believe, always without exception blessed. I hope you may be a thousand times more blessed among them than ever I was. Perhaps there are many souls that would never have been saved under my ministry, who may be touched under yours; and God has taken this method of bringing you into my place. *His name is Wonderful.*"

This done, and being already disengaged from his flock, he set out for London to make arrangements for the rest of the deputation, who soon after were all sent forth by the brethren with many prayers. None had more prayers offered in their behalf than he—and they were not offered in vain. During all his journeyings the Lord strengthened him, and saved him out of all distresses.

It was a singular event—often still it looks like a dream —that four ministers should be so suddenly called away from their quiet labours in the towns and villages of Scotland, and be found in a few weeks traversing the land of Israel, with their Bibles in their hand, eye-witnesses of prophecy fulfilled, and spies of the nakedness of Israel's worship and leanness of soul. The details of that journey need not be given here. They have been already recorded in the "Narrative of a Mission of Inquiry to the Jews, from the Church of Scotland, in 1839." But there are some incidents worthy to be preserved, which could find a place only in such a record of private life and feelings as we are now engaged in.

When Mr M'Cheyne was on board the vessel that carried him to London, he at once discovered an interesting young Jew, who seemed, however, unwilling to be recognized as belonging to the seed of Abraham. He made several attempts to draw this young Israelite into close conversation; and before parting, read with him the 1st Psalm in Hebrew, and pressed home the duty of meditating on the Word of the Lord. In visiting Bethnal Green, he has noted down that it was very sweet to hear Jewish children sing a hymn to Jesus, the burden of which was טָבוּחַ עָלֵינוּ "Slain for us!"

The awful profanation of the holy Sabbath which we witnessed on the streets of Paris, called forth the following appeal, in a letter to Mr Macdonald of Blairgowrie. His spirit had been stirred in him when he saw the city wholly given to idolatry. "Stand in the breach, dear friend, and lift up your voice like a trumpet, lest Scotland become another France. You know how many in our own parishes trample on the holy day. They do not know how sweet it is to walk with God all that holy day. Isaiah lviii. 11–14 is a sweet text to preach from. Exodus xxxi. 13 is also very precious, shewing that the real sanctifying of the Sabbath is one of God's signs or marks which he puts upon his people. It is one of the letters of the new name, which no one knoweth but they who receive it."

In his brief notes during the first part of the journey, he has seldom failed to mark our seasons of united prayer, such as those in the cabin of the vessel on the passage to Genoa; for these were times of refreshing to his spirit. And his feelings, as he stood in that city, and surveyed its palaces, are expressed in a few lines, which he sent homeward from the spot. "A foreign land draws us nearer God. He is the only one whom we know here. We go to him as to one we know: all else is strange. Every step I take, and every new country I see, makes me feel more that there is nothing real, nothing true, but what is everlasting. The whole world lieth in wickedness: its judgments are fast hastening. The marble palaces, among which I have been wandering to-night, shall soon sink like a millstone in the waters of God's righteous anger; but he that doeth the will of God abideth for ever."

At Valetta, in the island of Malta, he wrote—"My heart beats a little to-day, but another sail will do me good. One thing I know, that I am in the hands of my Father in heaven, who is all love to me—not for what I am in myself, but for the beauty he sees in Immanuel."

The classic shores of Italy and Greece are invested with a peculiar interest, such as may raise deep emotions even in a sanctified soul. "We tried to recollect many of the studies of our boyhood. But what is classic learning to us now? I count all things but loss for the excellency of the knowledge of Christ Jesus my Lord. And yet these recollections tinged every object, and afforded us a most lawful pleasure."

During our voyage, it was his delight to search into the Scriptures, just as at home. And so much did he calculate on an unceasing study of the Word during all our journey, that he took with him some notes I had written on each chapter of the Book of Leviticus, observing it would be suitable meditation for us while busy with Jewish minds. At home and abroad he had an insatiable appetite for all the Word—both for the types of the Old Testament, and the plain text of the New. On one occasion, before leaving home, in studying Numbers iv, he fixed the different duties assigned to the Priests on his memory, by means of the following lines:—

> "The *Kohathites* upon their shoulder bear
> The holy vessels, covered with all care;
> The *Gershonites* receive an easier charge,
> Two waggons full of cords and curtains large;
> *Merari's* sons four ponderous waggons load
> With boards and pillars of the house of God."

He acted on the principle that whatever God has revealed must deserve our study and prayerful investigation.

Arrived at Alexandria in Egypt, and thence proceeding onward to Palestine by the way of the desert, we found ourselves set down on a new stage of experience. Mr M'Cheyne observed on the silence of the desert places—"It is a remarkable feeling to be quite alone in a desert place; it gives similar feelings to fasting; it brings God near. Living in tents, and moving among such lonely scenes for many days, awake many new ideas. It is a strange life we lead in the wilderness. Round and round there is a complete circle of sand and wilderness-shrubs; above, a blue sky without a cloud, and a scorching sun which often made the thermometer stand at 96° in our tents. When evening came, the sun went down as it does in the ocean, and the stars came riding forth in their glory; and we used to pitch all alone, with none but our poor ignorant Bedouins and their camels, and our all-knowing, all-loving God beside us. When morning began to dawn, our habitations were taken down. Often we have found ourselves shelterless before being fully dressed. What a type of the tent of our body! Ah! how often taken down before the soul is made meet for the inheritance of the saints in light." To Mr Bonar of Larbert he writes: "I had no idea that travelling in the wilderness was so dreadful a thing as it is. The loneliness I often felt quite solemnized me. The burning sun overhead—round and round a circle of barren sand, chequered only by a few prickly shrubs ('the heath of the wilderness,' of which Jeremiah speaks)—no rain, not a cloud, the wells often like that of Marah, and far between. I now understand well the murmurings of Israel. I feel that our journey proved and tried my own heart very much." When we look back, and remember that he who thus stands on the sandy desert road between Egypt and Palestine, and looks on its singular scenery, is one who but lately was to be found busy night and day in dealing with the souls of men in the densely peopled streets of a town teeming with population, we are led to wonder at the ways of the Lord. But, is it not a moment which may remind us, that the God who sent Elijah to the brook at Cherith is the same God still? and that the wise, considerate, loving Master who said, "Come into a desert place and rest awhile," is as loving, considerate, and wise as he was then?

At Balteen, a small village in Egypt, I well remember the indignation that fired his countenance, when our Arab attendants insisted on travelling forward on the Sabbath-day, rather than continue sitting under a few palm-trees, breathing a sultry, furnace-like atmosphere, with nothing more than just such supply of food as sufficed. He could not bear the thought of being deprived of the Sabbath-rest; it was needful for our souls as much in the wilderness as in the crowded city; and if few glorify God in that desolate land, so much the more were we called on to fill these solitudes with our songs of praise. It was in this light he viewed our position; and when we had prevailed, and were seated under the palms, he was excited to deep emotion, though before quite unnerved by the heat, at the sight of a row of poor wretched Egyptians, who gathered round us. "O that I could speak their language, and tell them of salvation!" was his impassioned wish.

An event occurred at that time in which the hand of God afterwards appeared very plain, though it then seemed very dark to us. Dr Black fell from his camel in the midst of the sandy desert, and none of all our company could conjecture what bearing on the object of our Mission this sad occurrence could have. Is it a frown on our undertaking? or can it really be a movement of His kind, guiding hand? We often spoke of it; in our visit to Galilee we thought that we saw some purposes evolving; but there was still something unexplained. Now, however, the reason appears; even that event was of the Lord, in wise and kind design. But for that fall, our fathers in the deputation would not have sailed up the Danube on their way to Vienna, and Pesth would not have been visited. This accident, which mainly disabled Dr Black from undertaking the after fatigue of exploring Galilee, was the occasion of directing the steps of our two fathers to that station, where a severe stroke of sickness was made the means of detaining Dr Keith till they had learned that there was an open door among the Jews. And there, accordingly, it has been that the Lord has poured down his Spirit on the Jews that have come to our missionaries, so remarkably that no Jewish Mission seems ever to have been blessed with deeper conversions. There is nothing but truth in the remark made by one of our number:—"Dr Black's fall from the camel was the first step towards Pesth." "Whoso is wise, and will observe these things, even they shall understand the loving-kindness of the Lord;" Psalm cvii. 43. Indeed, whether it was that we were prepared to expect, and therefore were peculiarly ready to observe, or whether it was really the case that the watchful eye of our Lord specially guided us, certain it is that we thought we could perceive the whole course we took signally marked by Providence. There were many prayers in Scotland ascending up in our behalf, and the High Priest gave the answer by shining upon our path. Mr M'Cheyne has stated—"For much of our safety I feel indebted to the prayers of my people, I mean the Christians among them, who do not forget us. If the veil of the world's machinery were lifted off, how much we would find is done in answer to the prayers of God's children."

Many things lost somewhat of their importance in our view, when examined amid the undistracted reflections of the long desert journey, where for many days we had quiet, like the quiet of death, around us all night long, and even during the bright day. It is the more interesting, on this very account, to know his feelings there on the subject of the ministry. As his camel slowly bore him over the soft sandy soil, much did he ruminate on the happy days when he was permitted to use all his strength in preaching Jesus to dying men. "Use your health while you have it, my dear friend and brother. Do not cast away peculiar opportunities that may never come again. You know not when your last Sabbath with your people may come. Speak for eternity. Above all things, cultivate your own spirit. A word spoken by you when your conscience is clear, and your heart full of God's Spirit, is worth ten thousand words spoken in unbelief and sin. This was my great fault in the ministry. Remember it is God, and not man, that must have the glory. It is not much speaking, but much faith, that is needed. Do not forget us. Do not forget the Saturday night meeting, nor the Monday morning thanksgiving." Thus he wrote on his way to a fellow-labourer in Scotland.

On our first Sabbath in the Holy Land, our tent had been pitched in the vicinity of a colony of ants. It was in the tribe of Simeon we were encamped; it was the scenery of the Promised Land we had around us; and one of the similitudes of the blessed Word was illustrated within our view. He opened his Bible at Prov. vi. 6–8, and, as he read, noted—"I. *Consider her ways.* Most souls are lost for want of consideration. II. *The ant has no guide, overseer, or ruler;* no officer, no one to command or encourage her. How differently situated is the child of God! III. *Provideth her meat in the summer,* &c. Some have thought that this teaches us to heap up money; but quite the reverse. The ant lays up no store for the future. It is all for present use. She is always busy summer and winter. The lesson is one of constant diligence in the Lord's work."

Many a time in these days, when our attendants in the evening were driving in the stakes of our tent and stretching its cords, he would lie down on the ground under some tree that sheltered him from the dew. Completely exhausted by the long day's ride, he would lie almost speechless for half an hour; and then, when the palpitation of his heart had a little abated, would propose that we two should pray together. Often, too, did he say to me, when thus stretched on the ground—not impatiently, but very earnestly—"Shall I ever preach to my people again?" I was often reproved by his unabated attention to personal holiness; for this care was never absent from his mind, whether he was at home in his quiet chamber, or on the sea, or in the desert. Holiness in him was manifested, not by efforts to perform duty, but in a way so natural, that you recognized therein the easy outflowing of the indwelling Spirit. The fountain springing up unto everlasting life (John iv. 14) in his soul, welled forth its living waters alike in the familiar scenes of his native Scotland, and under the olive-trees of Palestine. Prayer and meditation on the Word were never forgotten; and a peace that the world could not give kept his heart and mind. When we were detained a day at Gaza, in very tantalizing circumstances, his remark was, *"Jehovah Jireh; we are at that mount again."* It was sweet at any time to be with him, for both nature and grace in him drew the very heart; but there were moments of enjoyment in these regions of Palestine that drew every cord still closer, and created unknown sympathies. Such was that evening when we climbed Samson's Hill together. Sitting there, we read over the references to the place in the Word of God; and then he took out his pencil and sketched the scene, as the sun was sinking in the West. This done, we sang some verses of a Psalm appropriate to the spot, offered up prayer, and, slowly descending, conversed of all we saw, and of all that was brought to mind by the scenery around us, till we reached our tent.

In approaching Jerusalem, we came up the Pass of Latroon. He writes, "The last day's journey to Jerusalem was the finest I ever had in all my life. For four hours we were ascending the rocky pass upon our patient camels. It was like the finest of our Highland scenes, only the trees and flowers, and the voice of the turtle, told us that it was Immanuel's land." Riding along, he remarked that to have seen the Plain of Judea and this mountain-pass was enough to reward us for all our fatigue; and then began to call up passages of the Old Testament Scriptures which might seem to refer to such scenery as that before us.

During our ten days at Jerusalem, there were few objects within reach that we did not eagerly seek to visit. "We stood at the turning of the road where Jesus came near, and beheld the city, and wept over it. And if we had had more of the mind that was in Jesus, I think we should have wept also." This was his remark in a letter homeward; and to Mr Bonar of Larbert, he expressed his feelings in regard to the Mount of Olives and its vicinity: "I remember, the day when I saw you last, you said, that there were other discoveries to be made than those in the physical world—that there were sights to be seen in the spiritual world, and depths to be penetrated, of far greater importance. I have often thought of the truth of your remark. But if there is a place on earth where physical scenery can help us to discover divine things, I think it is Mount Olivet. Gethsemane at your feet leads your soul to meditate on Christ's love and determination to undergo divine wrath for us. The cup was set before him there, and there he said, 'Shall I not drink it?' The spot where he wept makes you think of his divine compassion, mingling with his human tenderness—his awful justice, that would not spare the city—his superhuman love, that wept over its coming misery! Turning the other way, and looking to the south-east, you see Bethany, reminding you of his love to his own—that his name is love—that in all our afflictions he is afflicted—that those who are in their graves shall one day come forth at his command. A little farther down you see the Dead Sea, stretching far among the mountains its still and sullen waters. This deepens and solemnizes all, and makes you go away, saying, 'How shall we escape, if we neglect so great salvation?'"

He wrote to another friend in Scotland, from Mount Zion, where we were then dwelling.

"MOUNT ZION, *June* 12, 1839.

"MY DEAR FRIEND,—Now that we are in the most wonderful spot in all this world—where Jesus lived, and walked, and prayed, and died, and will come again—I doubt not you will be anxious to hear how we come on. I am thankful that ever he privileged us to come to this land. I heard of my flock yesterday by a letter from home—the first I have received, dated 8th May.   *   *   *   We are living in one of the missionaries' houses on Mount Zion. My window looks out upon where the Temple was, the beautiful Mount of Olives rising behind. The Lord that made heaven and earth bless thee out of Zion.—Yours," &c.

One evening, after our visit to Sychar, he referred to the Bible which I had dropped into Jacob's Well. We were then resting from our journey in our tents. Soon after, he penned on a leaf of his note-book the following fragment:—

"My own loved Bible, must I part from thee,
Companion of my toils by land and sea;
Man of my counsels, soother of distress,
Guide of my steps through this world's wilderness!
In darkest nights, a lantern to my feet;
In gladsome days, as dropping honey sweet.
When first I parted from my quiet home,
At thy command, for Israel's good to roam,
Thy gentle voice said, 'For Jerusalem pray,
So shall Jehovah prosper all thy way.'
When through the lonely wilderness we strayed,
Sighing in vain for palm-trees' cooling shade,
Thy words of comfort hushed each rising fear,
'The shadow of thy mighty Rock is near.'
And when we pitched our tent on Judah's hills,
Or thoughtful mused beside Siloa's rills;
Whene'er we climbed Mount Olivet, to gaze
Upon the sea, where stood in ancient days
The heaven-struck Sodom——
    Sweet record of the past, to faith's glad eyes,
    Sweet promiser of glories yet to rise!" [1]

At the foot of Carmel, during the seven days we were in quarantine under the brow of the hill, we had time to recall many former scenes; and in these circumstances he wrote the hymn, "*The Fountain of Siloam.*"

Here, too, he had leisure to write home; and most graphically does he describe our journey from Alexandria onward.

"CARMEL, *June* 26, 1839.

"MY DEAR FATHER, MOTHER, &c.—It is a long time since I have been able to write to you—this being the first time since leaving Egypt that any one has appeared to carry letters for us. I must, therefore, begin by telling you that, by the good hand of our God upon me, I am in excellent health, and have been ever since I wrote you last. Fatigues we have had many, and much greater than I anticipated; hardships and dangers we have also encountered, but God has brought us all safely through and in fully better condition than when we began. You must not imagine that I have altogether lost the palpitation of my heart, for it often visits me to humble and prove me; still I believe it is a good deal better than it was, and its visits are not nearly so frequent.

[1] It is a somewhat curious occurrence, that the remnants of this Bible were found, and drawn up from the bottom of the well, in July 1843, by Dr Wilson, and his fellow-traveller, who employed a Samaritan from Sychar to descend and examine the well.

I hope very much, that in a cold bracing climate, and with less fatigue, I may, perhaps, not feel it at all. I was very thankful to receive your letter, dated 8th May—the first since leaving home. I was delighted to hear of your health and safety, and of the peaceful communion at St Peter's. The public news was alarming and humbling.[1] I suppose I had better begin at the beginning, and go over all our journeyings from the land of Egypt through the howling wilderness, to this sweet land of promise. I would have written *journalwise* (as my mother would say) from time to time, so that I might have had an interesting budget of news ready; but you must remember it is a more fatiguing thing to ride twelve or fourteen hours on a camel's back, in a sandy wilderness, than in our home excursions; and I could often do nothing more than lie down on my rug and fall asleep.

"We left Alexandria on 16th May 1839, parting from many kind friends in that strange city. We and our baggage were mounted on seventeen donkeys, like the sons of Jacob, when they carried corn out of Egypt. Our saddle was our bedding, viz., a rug to lie on, a pillow for the head, and a quilt to wrap ourselves in. We afterwards added a straw mat to put below all. We had procured two tents—one large, and a smaller one which Andrew and I occupy. The donkeys are nice nimble little animals, going about five miles an hour; a wild Arab accompanies each donkey. We have our two Arab servants, to whom I now introduce you—Ibrahim, a handsome small-made Egyptian, and Achmet the cook, a dark good-natured fellow, with a white turban and bare black legs. Ibrahim speaks a little English and Italian, and Achmet, Italian—in addition to their native Arabic. I soon made friends with our Arab donkey-men, learning Arabic words and phrases from them, which pleased them greatly. We journeyed by the Bay of Aboukir, close by the sea, which tempered the air of the desert. At night we reached Rosetta, a curious half-inhabited eastern town. We saw an eastern marriage, which highly pleased us, illustrating the parables. It was by torch-light. We slept in the convent. 17th,—Spent

[1] He alludes here to the decision of the House of Lords in the Auchterarder case.

morning in Rosetta: gave the monk a New Testament. Saw some of Egyptian misery in the bazaar. Saw the people praying in the mosque, Friday being the Moslem's day of devotion. In the evening we crossed the Nile in small boats. It is a fine river; and its water, when filtered, is sweet and pleasant. We often thought upon it in the desert. We slept that night on the sand, in our tents, by the sea-shore. 18th,— In six hours we came to Bourlos (you will see it in the map of the Society for Diffusing Useful Knowledge): were ferried across. Watched the fishermen casting their nets into the sea: hot—hot. In two hours more, through a palmy wilderness, we came to Balteen—'the Vale of Figs'—an Arab village of mud huts. You little know what an Arab house is. In general, in Egypt, it is an exact square box, made of mud, with a low hole for a door. The furniture is a mat and cooking things; an oven made of mud. 19th,—Spent our Sabbath unoccupied in midst of the village; the poor Arabs have no Sabbath. The thermometer 84° in tent. The governor called in the evening, and drank a cup of tea with great relish. The heat we felt much all day; still it was sweet to rest and remember you all in the wilderness. 20th,— At twelve at night, left Balteen by beautiful moonlight. Proceeding through a pleasant African wild of palms and brushwood, we reached the sea in two hours, and rode along, its waves washing our feet—very sleepy. We got a rest at midday, if rest it could be called, under that scorching sun, which I never will forget. Proceeding onward, at three o'clock we left the sea-shore, and perceived the minarets of Damietta. Before us the mirage cheated us often when we were very thirsty. We crossed the Nile again, a much smaller branch—the only remaining one—and soon found ourselves comfortably reclining on the divan of the British Consul, an Egyptian gentleman of some fortune and manners. He entertained us at supper in true Egyptian style; provided a room for us, where we spread our mats in peace. We spent the whole of the next day here, having sent off a Bedouin to have camels ready for us at San. The Consul entertained us in the same Egyptian style of hospitality, and sent us away the next day on board a barge upon Lake

Menzaleh. 22nd,—Even E—— would not have been afraid to sail upon that lake. It is nowhere more than ten feet deep, and in general only four or five. We made an awning with our mats, and spent a very happy day. At evening we entered a canal among immense reeds. In moonlight the scene was truly romantic: we slept moored to the shore all night. Next morning (23rd) we reached San about ten. This evening and next morning we spent in exploring the ruins of the ancient Zoan, for this we find is the very spot.

"Wandering alone, we were quite surprised to find great mounds of brick, and pottery, and vitrified stone. Andrew at last came upon beautiful obelisks. Next morning we examined all carefully, and found two sphinxes and many Egyptian obelisks. How wonderful to be treading over the ruins of the ancient capital of Egypt! Isaiah xix. 12, 'Where are the princes of Zoan?' Ezek. xxx. 14, 'God has set fire in Zoan.' This is the very place where Joseph was sold as a slave, and where Moses did his wonders; Psalm lxxviii. 43. This was almost the only place where we have been in danger from the inhabitants. They are a wild race; and our Arabs were afraid of them. You would have been afraid too, if you had seen, out of the door of our tent, our Bedouins keeping watch all night with their naked sabres gleaming in the moonlight, firing off their guns now and then, and keeping up a low chant to keep one another awake. No evil happened to us, and we feel that many pray for us, and that God is with us. 24th,—This day our journeyings on camels commenced, and continued till we came to Jerusalem. It is a strange mode of conveyance. You have seen a camel kneeling; it is in this condition that you mount; suddenly it rises first on its fore feet, and then on its hind feet. It requires great skill to hold yourself on during this operation; one time I was thrown fair over its head, but quite unhurt. When you find yourself exalted on the hunch of a camel, it is somewhat of the feeling of an aeronaut, as if you were bidding farewell to sublunary things; but when he begins to move, with solemn pace and slow, you are reminded of your terrestrial origin, and that a wrong balance or turn to the side will soon bring you down from your giddy height. You have no stirrup, and generally only your bed for your saddle; you may either sit as on horseback, or as on a side-saddle—the latter is the pleasanter, though not the safer of the two. The camel goes about three miles an hour, and the step is so long that the motion is quite peculiar. You bend your head toward your knees every step. With a vertical sun above and a burning sand below, you may believe it is a very fatiguing mode of journeying. However, we thought of Rebecca and Abraham's servant (Gen. xxiv.), and listened with delight to the wild Bedouins' plaintive song. That night, 24th, we slept at Menagie, a Bedouin mud village—palm trees and three wells, and an ocean of sand, formed the only objects of interest. 25th,—Up by sunrise, and proceeded as before. The only event this day was Dr Black's fall from his camel, which greatly alarmed us. He had fallen asleep, which you are very apt to do; we encamped and used every restorative, so that we were able to proceed the same evening to Gonatre, a miserable Arab post, having a governor; not a tree. 26th—The Sabbath dawned sweetly; thermometer 92° in tent; could only lie on the mat and read Psalms. Evening—Gathered governor and Bedouins to hear some words of eternal life, Ibrahim interpreting. 27th,—Two very long stages brought us to Katieh; thankful to God for his goodness while we pitched by the date trees. 28th,—Spent the day at Katieh; interesting interviews with the governor, a kind Arab; thermometer 96° in tent. Same evening, proceeded through a greener desert, among flocks of goats and sheep, and encamped by a well, Bir-el-Abd. 29th,—Another hot day in the desert; came in sight of the sea, which gave us a refreshing breeze; bathed in a salt lake as hot as a warm-bath. Evening—Encampment at Abulgilbany. 30th,—This was our last day in the Egyptian wilderness. We entered on a much more mountainous region. The heat very great; we literally panted for a breath of wind. The Bedouins begged handkerchiefs to cover their heads, and often cast themselves under a bush for shade. Towards sunset, we came down to the old ruins of Rhinoculura, now buried in the sand; and soon after our camels kneeled down at the gates of El Arish, the last town on the Egyptian frontier. 31st,—We spent in El Arish, being unable to get fresh camels. We bought a sheep for five shillings; drank freely of their delightful water—What a blessing after the desert! Found out the river of Egypt, the boundary of Judah mentioned in the Bible, quite dry. 1st June,—Visited the school, a curiosity, all the children sit cross-legged on the floor, rocking to and fro, repeating something in Arabic. We had a curious interview with the governor, sitting in the gate in the ancient manner. We are quite expert now at taking off our shoes and sitting in the Eastern mode. Smoking, and coffee in very small cups, are the constant accompaniments of these visits. Left the same evening, and did not reach Sheikh Juidhe, in the land of the Philistines, till the sun was nearly bursting into view. 2nd,—Spent a happy Sabbath here; sung 'In Judah's land God is well known.' Singing praise in our tents is very sweet; they are so frail, like our mortal bodies; they rise easily into the ears of our present Father. Our journey through the land of the Philistines was truly pleasant. 3rd,—We went through a fine pasture country; immense straths; flocks of sheep and goats, and asses and camels, often came in sight. This is the very way up out of Egypt, little changed from the day that the Ethiopian went on his way rejoicing, and Joseph and Mary carried down the babe from the anger of Herod. Little changed! did I say? it is all changed; no more is there one brook of water. Every river of Egypt Wady Gaza, Eshcol, Sorek—every brook we crossed, was dried up, not a drop of water. The land is changed; no more is it the rich land of Philistia. The sand struggles with the grass for mastery. The cities are changed—where are they? The people are changed—no more the bold Philistines —no more the children of Simeon—no more Isaac and his herdsmen—no more David and his horsemen; but miserable Arab shepherds—simple people, without ideas—poor, degraded, fearful. Khanounes was the first town we entered —Scripture name unknown. The burying-ground outside the town. The well, and people coming to draw, were objects of great interest to us. The people were highly entertained with us in return. We sat down in the bazaar, and were a spectacle to all. How much we longed to have the Arabic tongue, that we might preach the unsearchable riches of Christ in God's own land. Same evening, we heard the cry of the wolf, and encamped two miles from Gaza. The plague was raging, so we did not enter, but spent a delightful day in comparing its condition with God's word concerning it—'Baldness is come upon Gaza.' The old city is buried under sand-hills, without a blade of grass, so that it is bald indeed. The herds and flocks are innumerable, fulfilling Zeph. ii.; Andrew and I climbed the hill up which Samson carried the gates. 5th,—Passed through a fine olive grove for many miles, and entered the vale of Eshcol. The people were all in the fields cutting and bringing in their barley. They reap with the hook as we do. They seem to carry in at the same time upon camels. No vines in Eshcol now—no pomegranates; but some green fig-trees. Crossed the brook Sorek—dry. Spent the mid-day under the embowering shade of a fig-tree; tasted the apricots of the good land. Same evening we came to Doulis, which we take to be Eshtaol, where Samson was born. 6th,—We went due east, and, after a mountain pass, saw the hills of Judah—an immense plain intervening, all studded with little towns. From their names, we found out many Bible spots. This valley or plain is the very vale of Zephatha, of which you read in 2 Chronicles chap. xiv.—'in the plain of Sephela.' Before night we entered among the hills of Judah—very like our own Highlands—and slept all night among the mountains, at a deserted village called Latroon. 7th,—One of the most privileged days of our life. We broke up our tents by moonlight; soon the sun was up; we entered a defile of the most romantic character; wild rocks and verdant hills—wild flowers of every colour and fragrance scented our path. Sometimes we came upon a clump of beautiful olive trees, then wild again. The turtle's voice was heard in the land, and singing birds of sweetest note. Our camels carried us up this pass for four hours; and our turbaned Bedouins added by their strange figures to the scene. The terracing of all the hills is the most remarkable feature of Judean scenery. Every foot of the rockiest mountains may, in this way, be covered with vines. We thought of Isaiah wandering here, and David and Solomon. Still all was wilderness. The hand of man had been actively employed upon every mountain, but where were these labourers now? Judah is gone into captivity before the enemy. There are few men left in the land; not a vine is there. 'The vine languisheth.' We came down upon Garieh, a village embosomed in figs and pomegranates. Ascending again, we came down into the valley of Elah, where David slew Goliath. Another long and steep ascent of a most rugged hill, brought us into a strange scene—a desert of sunburnt rocks. I had read of this, and knew that Jerusalem was near. I left my camel and went before, hurrying over the burning rocks. In about half an hour Jerusalem came in sight. 'How doth the city sit solitary that was full of people!' Is this the perfection of beauty? 'How hath the Lord covered the daughter of Zion with a cloud in his anger!' It is, indeed, very desolate. Read the two first chapters of Lamentations, and you have a vivid picture of our first sight of Jerusalem. We lighted off our camels within the Jaffa gate. Among those that crowded round us, we observed several Jews. I think I had better not attempt to tell you about Jerusalem. There is so much to describe, and I know not where to begin. The Consul, Mr Young, received us most kindly, provided us a house where we might spread our mats, and helped us in every way. Mr Nicolayson called the same evening and insisted on our occupying one of the mission-houses on Mount Zion. The plague is still in Jerusalem, so that we must keep ourselves in quarantine. The plague only communicates by contact, so that we are not allowed to touch any one, or let any one touch us. Every night we heard the mourners going about the streets with their dismal wailings for the dead. On Sabbath Mr Nicolayson read the prayers, and Dr Black preached from Isaiah ii. 2. Dr Keith in the evening. Three converted Jews were among the hearers. On Monday 10th, we visited the Sepulchre, and a painful sight, where we can find no traces of Calvary. Same evening rode up to the Mount of Olives; past Gethsemane, a most touching spot. Visited Sir Moses Montefiore, a Jew of London, encamped on Mount Olivet; very kind to us. 11th,—Went round the most of the places to be visited near Jerusalem—Rephaim, Gihon, Siloa's Brook 'that flowed fast by the Oracle of God'; the Pool of Siloam—the place where Jesus wept over the city; Bethany—of all places my favourite—the tombs of the Kings. Such a day we never spent in this world before. The climate is truly delightful—hot at mid-day, but delightful breezes at morn and even. 12th,—A business day, getting information about Jews. In the evening, walked to Acel-dama—a dreadful spot. Zion is ploughed like a field. I gathered some barley, and noticed cauliflowers, planted in rows. See Micah iii. 12. Jerusalem is, indeed, heaps. The quantities of rubbish would amaze you—in one place higher than the walls. 13th,—We went to Hebron, twenty miles south; Mr Nicolayson, his son, the Consul, and ladies accompanying us, all on mules and horses. Judah's cities are all waste. Except Bethlehem, we saw none but ruins till we reached Hebron. The vines are beautifully cultivated here, and make it a Paradise. The hills all terraced to the top. We spent a delightful evening and all next day. We met the Jews and had an interesting interview with them. We read Genesis xviii., and many other Bible passages, with great joy. Saw the mosque where the tomb of Abraham and Sarah is. 14th,—Returned by Bethlehem to Jerusalem. Bethlehem is a sweet village, placed on the top of a rocky hill—very white and dazzling. You see it on both sides of the hill. At Rachel's sepulchre you see Jerusalem on one hand and Bethlehem on the other, an interesting sight—six miles apart. On Sabbath we enjoyed the Lord's Supper in an upper chamber in Jerusalem. It was a time much to be remembered. Andrew preached in the evening from John xiv. 2, 3. 17th,—The plague has been increasing so that we think it better to depart. Last visit to Gethsemane, and Bethany, and Siloam. Evening,—Took farewell of all our friends in Jerusalem, with much sorrow you may believe. Went due north to Ramah, by Gibeon, and slept at Beer, again in our tent, in Benjamin. 19th,—Passed Bethel where Jacob slept. Passed through the rich and rocky defile of Ephraim, by Lebonah, to Sychar. You cannot believe what a delightsome land it is. We sought anxiously for the well where Jesus sat. Andrew alone found it, and lost his Bible in it. 20th,—Had a most interesting morning with the Jews at Sychar. Saw many of them; also the Samaritans, in their synagogue. Same evening visited Samaria, a wonderful place, and encamped at Sanor. 21st,—Arrived at Carmel, where we now are, encamped within two yards of the sea. We have been in quarantine here seven days, as there is no plague north of this. Several English are encamped here— Lord R., Lord H., &c. We have daily conversations sitting on the sand. We are not allowed to touch even the rope of a tent. Acre is in sight across the bay. We have delightful bathing. Tomorrow Lord H. leaves, and kindly offers to take this. Carmel's rocky brow is over us. We are all well and happy. On Monday, we propose leaving for Tiberias and Saphet. Soon we shall be in Beyrout, and on our way to Smyrna. Do not be anxious for me. Trust us to God, who goes with us where we go. I only pray that our mission may be blessed to Israel. Sir Moses M. has arrived, and pitched his tent within fifty yards of us. Kindest regards to all that inquire after me, not forgetting dear W.—Your affectionate son," &c.

When the two elder brethren of the deputation left us for Europe, we turned southward again from Beyrout, to visit the regions of Phœnicia and Galilee. Never did Mr M'Cheyne seem more gladsome than in gazing on these regions.

At Tyre, he remembered the request of an elder in the parish of Larbert, who had written to him before his departure, stating what he considered to be a difficulty in the ordinary expositions of the prophecies which speak of that renowned city. With great delight, he examined the difficulty on the spot; and it is believed that his testimony on such points as these, when it reached some men of sceptical views in that scene of his early labours, was not unblest.

From Saphet he writes:—"I sat looking down upon the Lake this morning for about an hour. It was just at our feet —the very water where Jesus walked, where he called his disciples, where he rebuked the storm, where he said, 'Children, have ye any meat?' after he rose from the dead. Jesus is the same still." To his early and familiar friend, Mr Somerville, he thus describes the same view:—"O what a view of the Sea of Galilee is before you, at your feet! It is above three hours' descent to the water's edge, and yet it looks as if you could run down in as many minutes. The lake is much larger than I had imagined. It is hemmed in by mountains on every side, sleeping as calmly and softly as if it had been the sea of glass which John saw in heaven. We tried in vain to follow the course of the Jordan running through it. True, there were clear lines, such as you see in the wake of a vessel, but then these did not go straight through the lake. The hills of Bashan are very high and steep, where they run into the lake. At one point, a man pointed out to us where the tombs in the rocks are, where the demoniacs used to live; and near it the hills were exactly what the Scriptures describe, 'a steep place,' where the swine ran down into the sea. On the north-east of the sea, Hermon rises very grand, intersected with many ravines full of snow."

The day we spent at the lake—at the very water-side—was ever memorable; it was so peculiarly sweet. We felt an indescribable interest even in lifting a shell from the shore of a sea where Jesus had so often walked. It was here that two of the beautiful hymns in *"The Songs of Zion"* were suggested to him. The one was, *"How pleasant to me,"* &c., the other, *"To yonder side"*; but the latter lay beside him unfinished till a later period.

His complaint was now considerably abated; his strength seemed returning; and often did he long to be among his people again, though quieting his soul upon the Lord. Not a few pastors of another church, have, from time to time, come forth to this land, compelled by disease to seek for health in foreign regions; but how rarely do we find the pastor's heart retained—how rarely do we discover that the shepherd yearns still over the flock he left. But so deep were Mr M'Cheyne's feelings toward the flock over which the Holy Ghost had made him overseer, that his concern for them became a temptation to his soul. It was not in the mere desire to preach again that he manifested this concern; for this desire might have been selfish, as he said—"No doubt there is pride in this anxiety to preach; a submissive soul would rejoice only in doing the present will of God." But his prayers for them went up daily to the throne. We had precious sessions of united prayer also for that same end— especially one morning at sunrise in Gethsemane, and another morning at Carmel, where we joined in supplication on the silent shore at the foot of the hill as soon as day dawned, and then again at evening on the top, where Elijah prayed.

Distance of place, or peculiarities of circumstances, never altered his views of duty, nor changed his feelings as a minister of Christ. In Galilee he meditated upon the aspect of ecclesiastical affairs in our beloved Scotland, and the principles he had maintained appeared to him as plainly accordant with the Word of God when tried there, apart from excitement, as they did when he reviewed them in connection with their effect at home. "I hope," were his words to a brother in the ministry, 'I hope the Church has been well guided and blessed; and if times of difficulty are to come, I do believe there is no position so proper for her to be in, as the attitude of a missionary church, giving freely to Jew and Gentile, as she has freely received—so may she be found when the Lord comes."

At the foot of Lebanon, in the town of Beyrout, he was able to expound a chapter (Acts x.) at a prayer-meeting of the American brethren. This quite rejoiced his heart; for it seemed as if the Lord were restoring him, and meant again to use him in preaching the glad tidings. But shortly after, during the oppressive heat of the afternoon, he felt himself unwell. He had paid a visit to a young man from Glasgow in the town, who was ill of fever; and it is not unlikely that this visit, at a time when he was in a state of debility from previous fatigue, was the immediate occasion of his own illness. He was very soon prostrated under the fever. But his medical attendant apprehended no danger, and advised him to proceed to Smyrna, in the belief that the cool air of the sea would be much more in his favour than the sultry heat of Beyrout. Accordingly, in company with our faithful Hebrew friend, Erasmus Calman, we embarked; but as we lay off Cyprus, the fever increased to such a height, that he lost his memory for some hours, and was racked with excessive pain in his head. When the vessel sailed, he revived considerably, but during three days no medical aid could be obtained. He scarcely ever spoke; and only once did he for a moment, on a Saturday night, lift his languid eye, as he lay on deck enjoying the breeze, to catch a distant sight of Patmos. We watched him with agonizing anxiety till we reached Smyrna and the village of Bouja. Though three miles off, yet for the sake of medical aid he rode to this village upon a mule after sunset, ready to drop every moment with pain and burning fever. But here the Lord had prepared for him the best and kindest help. The tender and parental care of Mr and Mrs Lewis, in whose house he found a home, was never mentioned by him but with deepest gratitude; and the sight of the flowering jessamine, or the mention of the deep-green cypress, would invariably call up in his mind associations of Bouja and its inmates. He used to say it was his second birth-place.

During that time, like most of God's people who have been in sickness, he felt that a single passage of the Word of God was more truly food to his fainting soul than anything besides. One day his spirit revived, and his eye glistened, when I spoke of the Saviour's sympathy, adducing as the very words of Jesus, Psalm xli. 1—"*Blessed is he that considereth the poor, the Lord will deliver him in time of trouble*," &c. It seemed so applicable to his own case, as a minister of the glad tidings; for often had he "considered the poor," carrying a cup of cold water to a disciple. Another passage, written for the children of God in their distress, was spoken to him when he seemed nearly insensible—"*Call upon me in the day of trouble*." This word of God was as the drop of honey to Jonathan.

He himself thus spoke of his illness to his friends at home: —"I left the foot of Lebanon when I could hardly see, or hear, or speak, or remember; I felt my faculties going, one by one, and I had every reason to expect that I would soon be with my God. It is a sore trial to be alone and dying, in a foreign land, and it has made me feel, in a way that I never knew before, the necessity of having unfeigned faith in Jesus and in God. Sentiments, natural feelings, glowing fancies of divine things, will not support the soul in such an hour. There is much self-delusion in our estimation of ourselves when we are untried and in the midst of Christian friends, whose warm feelings give a glow to ours, which they do not possess in themselves." Even then he had his people in his heart. "When I got better, I used to creep out in the evenings about sunset. I often remembered you all then. I could not write, as my eyes and head were much affected; I could read but very little; I could speak very little, for I had hardly any voice; and so I had all my time to lay my people before God, and pray for a blessing on them. About the last evening I was there, we all went to the vintage, and I joined in gathering the grapes." To Mr Somerville he wrote:—"My mind was very weak when I was at the worst, and therefore the things of eternity were often dim. *I had no fear to die, for Christ had died*. Still I prayed for recovery, if it was the Lord's will. You remember you told me to be humble among your last advices. You see God is teaching me the same thing. I fear I am not thoroughly humbled. I feel the pride of my heart, and bewail it." To his kind medical friend Dr Gibson, in Dundee, he wrote:—"I really believed that my Master had called me home, and that I would sleep beneath the dark green cypresses of Bouja till the Lord shall come, and they that sleep in Jesus come with him; and my most earnest prayer was for my dear flock, that God would give them a pastor after his own heart."

When we met, after an eight days' separation, on board the vessel at Constantinople, he mentioned as one of the most interesting incidents of the week, that one evening, while walking with Mr Lewis, they met a young Greek and his wife, both of whom were believed to be really converted souls. It created a thrill in his bosom to meet with these almost solitary representatives of the once-faithful and much-tried native Church of Smyrna.

Meanwhile there were movements at home that proved the Lord to be he who "alone doeth wondrous things." The cry of his servant in Asia was not forgotten; the eye of the Lord turned towards his people. It was during the time of Mr M'Cheyne's sore sickness that his flock in Dundee were receiving blessing from the opened windows of heaven. Their pastor was lying at the gate of death, in utter helplessness. But the Lord had done this on very purpose; for he meant to show that he needed not the help of any: he could send forth new labourers, and work by new instruments, when it pleased him. We little knew that during the days when we were waiting at the foot of Lebanon for a vessel to carry us to Smyrna, the arm of the Lord had begun to be revealed in Scotland. On the 23rd of July the great Revival at Kilsyth took place.

Mr W. C. Burns, the same who was supplying Mr M'Cheyne's place in his absence, was on that day preaching to his father's flock; and while pressing upon them immediate acceptance of Christ with deep solemnity, the whole of the vast assembly were overpowered. The Holy Spirit seemed to come down as a rushing mighty wind, and to fill the place. Very many were that day struck to the heart; the sanctuary was filled with distressed and enquiring souls. All Scotland heard the glad news that the sky was no longer as brass—that the rain had begun to fall. The Spirit in mighty power began to work from that day forward in many places of the land.

Mr Burns returned to Mr M'Cheyne's flock on August 8th—one of the days when Mr M'Cheyne was stretched on his bed, praying for his people under all his own suffering. The news of the work at Kilsyth had produced a deep impression in Dundee; and two days after, the Spirit began to work in St Peter's, at the time of the prayer-meeting in the church, in a way similar to Kilsyth. Day after day, the people met for prayer and hearing the Word; and the times of the Apostles seemed returned, when "the Lord added to the Church daily of such as should be saved." All this time, Mr M'Cheyne knew not how gracious the Lord had been in giving him his heart's desire. It was not till we were within sight of home, that the glad news of these Revivals reached our ears. But he continued like Epaphras, "labouring fervently in prayer," and sought daily to prepare himself for a more efficient discharge of his office, should the Lord restore him to it again. He sends home this message to a fellow-labourer: "Do not forget to carry on the work in hearts brought to a Saviour. I feel this was one of my faults in the ministry. Nourish babes; comfort downcast believers; counsel those perplexed; perfect that which is lacking in their faith. Prepare them for sore trials. I fear most Christians are quite unready for days of darkness." (Mr Moody Stuart.)

Our journey led us through Moldavia, Wallachia, and Austria—lands of darkness and of the shadow of death. Profound strangers to the truth as it is in Jesus, the people of these lands, nevertheless, profess to be Christians. Superstition and its idolatries veil the glorious Object of faith from every eye. In these regions, as well as in those already traversed, Mr M'Cheyne's anxiety for souls appeared in the efforts he made to leave at least a few words of Scripture with the Jews whom we met, however short the time of our interview. His spirit was stirred in him; and, with his Hebrew Bible in his hand, he would walk up thoughtfully and solemnly to the first Jew he could get access to, and begin by calling the man's attention to some statement of God's Word. In Palestine, if the Jew did not understand Italian, he would repeat to him such texts in Hebrew as, "In that day there shall be a fountain opened to the house of David," &c. (Zech. xiii. 1.) And one evening, at the well of Doulis, when the Arab population were all clustered round the water troughs, he looked on very wistfully, and said, "If only we had Arabic, we might sow beside all waters!"

At Jassy, after a deeply interesting day spent in conversation with Jews who came to the inn, he said, "I will remember the faces of those men at the Judgment-seat." When he came among the more educated Jews of Europe, he rejoiced to find that they could converse with him in Latin. His heart was bent on doing what he could (Mark xiv. 8) in season and out of season. "One thing," he writes, "I am

deeply convinced of, that God can make the simplest statement of the gospel effectual to save souls. If only it be the
true gospel, the good tidings, the message that God loved the
world, and provided a ransom free to all, then God is able
to make it wound the heart, and heal it too. There is deep
meaning in the words of Paul, 'I am not ashamed of the
gospel of Christ.' "

The abominations of Popery witnessed in Austrian Poland,
called forth many a prayer for the destruction of the Man of
Sin. "The images and idols by the wayside are actually
frightful, stamping the whole land as a kingdom of darkness.
I do believe that a journey through Austria would go far to
cure some of the Popery-admirers of our beloved land." He
adds—"These are the marks of the beast upon this land."
And in like manner our privileges in Scotland used to appear
to him the more precious, when, as at Brody, we heard of
Protestants who were supplied with sermon only once a year.
"I must tell this to my people," said he, "when I return, to
make them prize their many seasons of grace."

He estimated the importance of a town or country by its
relation to the house of Israel; and his yearnings over these
lost sheep resembled his bowels of compassion for his flock
at home. At Tarnapol, in Galicia, he wrote home—"We are
in Tarnapol, a very nice clean town, prettily situated on a
winding stream, with wooded hills around. I suppose you
never heard its name before; neither did I till we were there
among Jews. I know not whether it has been the birthplace
of warriors, or poets, or orators; its flowers have hitherto
been born to blush unseen, at least by us barbarians of the
north; but if God revive the dry bones of Israel that are
scattered over the world, there will arise from this place an
exceeding great army."

Our friend and brother in the faith, Erasmus Calman,
lightened the tediousness of a long day's journey, by repeating to us some Hebrew poetry. One piece was on Israel's
present state of degradation; it began—

צוּר · גּוֹאֵל ·

מַהֵר וְחִישׁ פְּדוּת

As the vehicle drove along, we translated it line by line, and soon after Mr M'Cheyne put it into verse. The following lines are a part :—

> Rock and Refuge of my soul,
> Swiftly let the season roll,
> When thine Israel shall arise
> Lovely in the nations' eyes !
>
> Lord of glory, Lord of might,
> As our ransomed fathers tell;
> Once more for thy people fight,
> Plead for thy loved Israel.
> Give our spoilers' towers to be
> Waste and desolate as we.
>
> Hasten, Lord, the joyful year,
> When thy Zion, tempest-tossed,
> Shall the silver trumpet hear;
> Bring glad tidings to the lost !
> Captive, cast thy cords from thee,
> Loose thy neck—be free—be free !
>
> Why dost thou behold our sadness?
> See the proud have torn away
> All our years of solemn gladness,
> When thy flock kept holy-day !
> Lord, thy fruitful vine is bare,
> Not one gleaning grape is there !
>
> Rock and Refuge of my soul,
> Swiftly let the season roll,
> When thine Israel shall be,
> Once again, beloved and free !

In his notes, he has one or two subjects marked for hymns. One of these is—Isaiah ii. 3—"Come ye," &c., *a loving call to the Jews*. Another is to the same effect—Isaiah i. 15—"Come, let us reason together." But these he never completed. In Cracow, having heard of the death of a friend, the wife of an English clergyman, in the midst of her days and in the full promise of usefulness, he began to pen a few sweet lines of comfort.

> Oft as she taught the little maids of France
> To leave the garland, castanet, and dance,
> And listen to the words which she would say
> About the crowns that never fade away,
> A new expression kindled in her eye,
> A holy brightness, borrowed from the sky.
> And when returning to her native land,
> She bowed beneath a Father's chast'ning hand;

When the quick pulse and flush upon the cheek,
A touching warning to her friends would speak,
A holy cheerfulness yet filled her eye,
   Willing she was to live, willing to die.
As the good Shunammite (the Scriptures tell),
When her son died, said meekly, "It is well,"
So when Sophia lost her infant boy,
And felt how dear-bought is a mother's joy,
When with green turf the little grave she spread,
"Not lost, but gone before," she meekly said.
And now they sleep together 'neath the willow,
The same dew drops upon their silent pillow.
Return, O mourner, from this double grave,
And praise the God who all her graces gave.
Follow her faith, and let her mantle be
A cloak of holy zeal to cover thee.

The danger which he incurred from the shepherds in this region, and other similar perils to which he was exposed in company with others, have been recorded in the Narrative. Out of them all the Lord delivered him; and not from these perils only did he save him, but from many severe trials to his health, to which variety of climate and discomforts of accommodation subjected him. And now we were traversing Prussia, drawing nearer our own land. It was about five months since we had received letters from Scotland, our route having led us away from places which we had anticipated visiting, and where communications had been left for us. We pressed homeward somewhat anxiously, yet wondering often at past mercies. In a letter from Berlin, Mr M'Cheyne remarked, "Our heavenly Father has brought us through so many trials and dangers that I feel persuaded he will yet carry us to the end. Like John, we shall fulfil our course. 'Are there not twelve hours in the day?' Are we not all immortal till our work is done!" His strength was rapidly increasing; the journey had answered the ends anticipated to a great extent, in his restoration to health. He was able to preach at Hamburg to the English congregation of Mr Rheder, from whom it was that the first hint of a Revival in Dundee reached his ears. He heard just so much both of Kilsyth and Dundee as to make him long to hear more. A few days after, on board the vessel that conveyed us to England, he thus expressed his feelings:—

"MY DEAR FATHER AND MOTHER,—You will be glad to see by the date that we are once more in sight of the shores of happy England. I only wish I knew how you all are. I have not heard of you since I was in Smyrna. In vain did I enquire for letters from you at Cracow, Berlin, and Hamburg. You must have written to Warsaw, and the Resident there has not returned them to Berlin, as we desired. Andrew and I and Mr Calman are all quite well, and thankful to God, who has brought us through every danger in so many countries. I trust our course has not been altogether fruitless, and that we may now resign our commission with some hope of good issuing from it to the Church and to Israel. I preached last Sabbath in Hamburg, for the first time since leaving England, and felt nothing the worse of it; so that I do hope it is my heavenly Father's will to restore me to usefulness again among my beloved flock. We have heard something of a reviving work at Kilsyth. We saw it noticed in one of the newspapers. I also saw the name of Dundee associated with it; so that I earnestly hope good has been doing in our Church, and the dew from on high watering our parishes, and that the flocks whose pastors have been wandering may also have shared in the blessing. We are quite ignorant of the facts, and you may believe we are anxious to hear. . . . . We are now passing Woolwich, and in an hour will be in London. We are anxious to be home, but I suppose will not get away till next week. I never thought to have seen you again in this world, but now I hope to meet you once more in peace.—Believe me, your affectionate Son," &c.

The day we arrived on the shores of our own land was indeed a singular day. We were intensely anxious to hear of events that had occurred at home a few months before—the outpouring of the Spirit from on high—while our friends were intensely interested in hearing tidings of the Land of Israel and the scattered tribes. The reception of the deputation on their return, and the fruits of their mission, are well known, and have been elsewhere recorded.

Mr M'Cheyne listened with deepest interest to the

accounts given of what had taken place in Dundee during the month of August, when he lay at the gates of death in Bouja. The Lord had indeed fulfilled his hopes, and answered his prayers. His assistant, Mr Burns, had been honoured of God to open the flood-gate at Dundee, as well as at Kilsyth. For some time before, Mr Burns had seen symptoms of deeper attention than usual, and of real anxiety in some that had hitherto been careless. But it was after his return from Kilsyth that the people began to melt before the Lord. On Thursday, the second day after his return, at the close of the usual evening prayer-meeting in St Peter's, and when the minds of many were deeply solemnized by the tidings which had reached them, he spoke a few words about what had for some days detained him from them, and invited those to remain who felt the need of an outpouring of the Spirit to convert them. About a hundred remained; and at the conclusion of a solemn address to these anxious souls, suddenly the power of God seemed to descend, and all were bathed in tears. At a similar meeting, next evening, in the church, there was much melting of heart and intense desire after the Beloved of the Father; and on adjourning to the vestry, the arm of the Lord was revealed. No sooner was the vestry-door opened to admit those who might feel anxious to converse, than a vast number pressed in with awful eagerness. It was like a pent-up flood breaking forth; tears were streaming from the eyes of many, and some fell on the ground groaning, and weeping, and crying for mercy. Onward from that evening, meetings were held every day for many weeks; and the extraordinary nature of the work justified and called for extraordinary services. The whole town was moved. Many believers doubted; the ungodly raged; but the Word of God grew mightily and prevailed. Instances occurred where whole families were affected at once, and each could be found mourning apart, affording a specimen of the times spoken of by Zechariah (xii. 12). Mr Baxter of Hilltown, Mr Hamilton, then assistant at Abernyte, and other men of God in the vicinity, hastened to aid in the work. Mr Roxburgh of St John's, and Mr Lewis of St David's, examined the work impartially and judiciously, and testified it to be of God. Dr M'Donald of Ferintosh, a man of God well experienced in Revivals, came to the spot and put to his seal also; and continued in town, preaching in St David's Church to the anxious multitudes, during ten days. How many of those who were thus awfully awakened were really brought to the truth, it was impossible to ascertain. When Mr M'Cheyne arrived, drop after drop was still falling from the clouds.

Such in substance were the accounts he heard before he reached Dundee. They were such as made his heart rejoice. He had no envy at another instrument having been so honoured in the place where he himself had laboured with many tears and temptations. In true Christian magnanimity, he rejoiced that the work of the Lord was done, by whatever hand. Full of praise and wonder, he set his foot once more on the shore of Dundee.

CHAPTER V

DAYS OF REVIVAL

"They shall spring up as *among the grass, as willows by the water courses."*—ISAIAH xliv. 4.

HIS people, who had never ceased to pray for him, welcomed his arrival among them with the greatest joy. He reached Dundee on a Thursday afternoon; and in the evening of the same day—being the usual time for prayer in St Peter's —after a short meditation, he hastened to the church, there to render thanks to the Lord, and to speak once more to his flock. The appearance of the church that evening, and the aspect of the people, he never could forget. Many of his brethren were present to welcome him, and to hear the first words of his opened lips. There was not a seat in the church unoccupied, the passages were completely filled, and the stairs up to the pulpit were crowded, on the one side with the aged, on the other with eagerly-listening children. Many a face was seen anxiously gazing on their restored pastor;

many were weeping under the unhealed wounds of conviction; all were still and calm, intensely earnest to hear. He gave out Psalm lxvi., and the manner of singing, which had been remarked since the Revival began, appeared to him peculiarly sweet—"so tender and affecting, as if the people felt that they were praising a present God." After solemn prayer with them, he was able to preach for above an hour. Not knowing how long he might be permitted to proclaim the glad tidings, he seized that opportunity, not to tell of his journeyings, but to shew the way of life to sinners. His subject was 1 Cor. ii. 1–4—the matter, the manner, and the accompaniments of Paul's preaching. It was a night to be remembered.

On coming out of the church, he found the road to his house crowded with old and young, who were waiting to welcome him back. He had to shake hands with many at the same time; and before this happy multitude would disperse, had to speak some words of life to them again, and pray with them where they stood. "To thy name, O Lord," said he that night, when he returned to his home, "To thy name, O Lord, be all the glory." A month afterwards, he was visited by one who had hitherto stood out against all the singular influence of the Revival, but who that night was deeply awakened under his words, so that the arrow festered in her soul, till she came crying, "O my hard, hard heart!"

On the Sabbath, he preached to his flock in the afternoon. He chose 2 Chron. v. 13, 14, as his subject; and in the close, his hearers remember well how affectionately and solemnly he said—"Dearly beloved and longed for, I now begin another year of my ministry among you; and I am resolved, if God give me health and strength, that I will not let a man, woman, or child among you alone, until you have at least heard the testimony of God concerning his Son, either to your condemnation or salvation. And I will pray, as I have done before, that, if the Lord will indeed give us a great outpouring of his Spirit, he will do it in such a way that it will be evident to the weakest child among you, that it is the Lord's work, and not man's. I think I may say to you, as Rutherford said to his people, 'Your heaven would be two heavens to me.' And if the Lord be pleased to give me a crown from among you, I do here promise in his sight, that I will cast it at his feet, saying, 'Worthy is the Lamb that was slain! Blessing, and honour, and glory, and power, be unto Him that sitteth upon the throne, and to the Lamb, for ever and ever.' "

It was much feared for a time, that a jealous spirit would prevail among the people of St Peter's, some saying, "I am of Paul, and others, I of Cephas." Those recently converted were apt to regard their spiritual father in a light in which they could regard none besides. But Mr M'Cheyne had received from the Lord a holy disinterestedness that suppressed every feeling of envy. Many wondered at the singleheartedness he was enabled to exhibit. He could sincerely say, "I have no desire but the salvation of my people, by whatever instrument."

Never, perhaps, was there one placed in better circumstances for testing the Revival impartially, and seldom has any Revival been more fully tested. He came among a people whose previous character he knew; he found a work wrought among them during his absence, in which he had not had any direct share; he returned home to go out and in among them, and to be a close observer of all that had taken place; and, after a faithful and prayerful examination, he did most unhesitatingly say, that the Lord had wrought great things, whereof he was glad; and, in the case of many of those whose souls were saved in that Revival, he discovered remarkable answers to the prayers of himself, and of those who had come to the truth, before he left them. He wrote to me his impressions of the work, when he had been a few weeks among his people:—

"2nd Dec., 1839.

"Rev. And. A. Bonar, Collace.

"My dear A.—I begin upon note-paper, because I have no other on hand but our thin travelling paper. I have much to tell you, and to praise the Lord for. I am grieved to hear that there are no marks of the Spirit's work about Collace during your absence; but if Satan drive you to your knees, he will soon find cause to repent it. Remember how fathers do to their children when they ask bread. How much more shall our heavenly Father give (*ἀγαθά*) all good things to them that ask him. Remember the rebuke which I once got from old Mr Dempster of Denny, after preaching to his people—'I was highly pleased with your discourse, but in prayer it struck me that you thought God *unwilling to give.*' Remember Daniel—'At the beginning of thy supplications the commandment came forth.' And do not think you are forgotten by me as long as I have health and grace to pray.

"Every thing here I have found in a state better than I expected. The night I arrived I preached to such a congregation as I never saw before. I do not think another person could have got into the church, and there was every sign of the deepest and tenderest emotion. R. Macdonald was with me, and prayed. Affliction and success in the ministry have taught and quickened him. I preached on I Cor. ii. 1–4, and felt what I have often heard, that it is easy to preach where the Spirit of God is. On the Friday night Mr Burns preached. On the Sabbath I preached on that wonderful passage, 2 Chron. v. 13, 14; Mr Burns preached twice, morning and evening. His views of Divine truth are clear and commanding. There is a great deal of substance in what he preaches, and his manner is very powerful,—so much so, that he sometimes made me tremble. In private, he is deeply prayerful, and seems to feel his danger of falling into pride.

"I have seen many of the awakened, and many of the saved; indeed, this is a pleasant place compared with what it was once. Some of the awakened are still in the deepest anxiety and distress. Their great error is exactly what your brother Horace told me. They think that coming to Christ is some strange act of their mind, different from believing what God has said of his Son; so much so, that they will tell you with one breath, I believe all that God has said, and yet with the next, complain that they cannot come to Christ, or close with Christ. It is very hard to deal with this delusion.

"I find some old people deeply shaken; they feel insecure. One confirmed drunkard has come to me, and is, I believe, now a saved man. Some little children are evidently saved.

All that I have yet seen are related to converts of my own. One, eleven years old, is a singular instance of Divine grace. When I asked if she desired to be made holy, she said, 'Indeed, I often wish I was awa', that I might sin nae mair.' A. L. of fifteen, is a fine tender-hearted believer. W. S., ten, is also a happy boy.

"Many of my own dear children in the Lord are much advanced; much more full of joy—their hearts lifted up in the ways of the Lord. I have found many more savingly impressed under my own ministry than I knew of. Some have come to tell me. In one case, a whole family saved. I have hardly met with any thing to grieve me. Surely the Lord hath dealt bountifully with me. I fear, however, that the great Spirit has in some measure passed by—I hope soon to return in greater power than ever. The week meetings are thinner now. I will turn two of them into my classes soon, and so give solid, regular instruction, of which they stand greatly in need. I have not met with one case of extravagance or false fire, although doubtless there may be many. At first, they used to follow in a body to our house, and expected many an address and prayer by the road. They have given up this now. I preached last Sabbath twice, first on Isaiah xxviii. 14–18, and then on Rev. xii. 11, 'Overcame by the blood of the Lamb.' It was a very solemn day. The people willingly sat till it was dark. Many make it a place of Bochim. Still there is nothing of the power which has been. I have tried to persuade Mr Burns to stay with us, and I think he will remain in Dundee. I feel fully stronger in body than when I left you. Instead of exciting me, there is everything to solemnize and still my feelings. Eternity sometimes seems very near.

"I would like your advice about prayer-meetings;—how to consolidate them; what rules should be followed, if any; whether there should be mere reading of the Word and prayer, or free converse also on the passage? We began to-day a ministerial prayer-meeting, to be held every Monday at eleven for an hour and a half. This is a great comfort, and may be a great blessing. Of course, we do not invite the colder ministers; that would only damp our meeting. Tell me if you think this right.

"And now, dear A., I must be done, for it is very late. May your people share in the quickening that has come over Dundee! I feel it a very powerful argument with many—'Will you be left dry when others are getting drops of heavenly dew?' Try this with your people.

"I think it probable we shall have another communion again before the regular one. It seems very desirable. You will come and help us; and perhaps Horace too.

"I thought of coming back by Collace from Errol, if our Glasgow meeting had not come in the way.

"Will you set agoing your Wednesday meeting again immediately?

"Farewell, dear A. 'O man, greatly beloved, fear not; peace be to thee; be strong; yea, be strong.' Yours ever," &c.

To Mr Burns he thus expresses himself, on December 19th:—"My dear Brother, I shall never be able to thank you for all your labours among the precious souls committed to me; and what is worse, I can never thank God fully for his kindness and grace, which every day appears to me more remarkable. He has answered prayer to me in all that has happened, in a way which I have never told any one." Again, on the 31st, "Stay where you are, dear brother, as long as the Lord has any work for you to do.[1] If I know my own heart, its only desire is that Christ may be glorified, by souls flocking to him, and abiding in him, and reflecting his image; and whether it be in Perth or Dundee, should signify little to us. You know I told you my mind plainly, that I thought the Lord had so blessed you in Dundee, that you were called to a fuller and deeper work there; but if the Lord accompanies you to other places, I have nothing to object. The Lord strengthened my body and soul last Sabbath, and my spirit also was glad. The people were much

---

[1] Mr Burns was at that time in Perth, and there had begun to be some movement among the dry bones.

alive in the Lord's service. But O, dear brother, the most are Christless still. The rich are almost untroubled."

His evidence on this subject is given fully in his answers to the queries put by a Committee of the Aberdeen Presbytery; and, in a note to a friend, he incidentally mentions a pleasing result of this wide-spread awakening. "I find many souls saved under my own ministry, whom I never knew of before. They are not afraid to come out now, it has become so common a thing to be concerned about the soul." At that time, also, many came from a distance—one came from the north, who had been a year in deep distress of soul, to seek Christ in Dundee.

In his brief diary he records, on December 3rd, that twenty anxious souls had that night been conversing with him; "many of them very deeply interesting." He occasionally fixed an evening for the purpose of meeting with those who were awakened; and in one of his note-books there are at least *four hundred* visits recorded, made to him by inquiring souls, in the course of that and the following years. He observed that those who had been believers formerly had got their hearts enlarged, and were greatly established; and some seemed able to feed upon the truth in a new manner—as when one related to him, how there had for some time appeared a glory in the reading of the Word in public, quite different from reading it alone.

At the same time he saw backslidings, both among those whom believers had considered really converted, and among those who had been deeply convicted, though never reckoned among the really saved. He notes in his book—"Called to see ——. Poor lad, he seems to have gone back from Christ, led away by evil company. And yet I felt sure of him at one time. What blind creatures ministers are! man looketh at the outward appearance." One morning he was visited by one of his flock, proposing "a concert for prayer on the following Monday, in behalf of those who had fallen back, that God's Spirit might re-awaken them,"—so observant were the believers as well as their pastor of declensions. Among those who were awakened, but never truly converted, he mentions one case. "January 9. 1840.—Met with the case of one who had been frightened during the late work, so that her bodily health was injured. She seems to have no care now about her soul. It has only filled her mouth with evil-speaking."

That many, who promised fair, drew back and walked no more with Jesus, is true. Out of about 800 souls, who, during the months of the Revival, conversed with different ministers in apparent anxiety, no wonder surely if many proved to have been impressed only for a time. President Edwards considered it likely that, in such cases, the proportion of real conversions might resemble the proportion of blossoms in spring, and fruit in autumn. Nor can anything be more unreasonable than to doubt the truth of all, because of the deceit of some. The world itself does not so act in judging of its own. The world reckons upon the possibility of being mistaken in many cases, and yet does not cease to believe that there is honesty and truth to be found. One of themselves, a poet of their own, has said with no less justice than beauty—

> "Angels are bright still, though the brightest fell;
> And though foul things put on the brows of grace,
> Yet grace must still look so."

But, above all, we have the authority of the word of God, declaring that such backslidings are the very tests of the true Church—"For there must be also heresies among you, that they which are approved may be made manifest among you." 1 Cor. xi. 19. It is not, however, meant that any who had really believed went back to perdition. On the contrary, it is the creed of every sound evangelical church that those who do go back to perdition were persons who never really believed in Jesus. Their eyes may have been opened to see the dread realities of sin and of the wrath to come, but if they saw not righteousness for their guilty souls in the Saviour, there is nothing in all Scripture to make us expect that they will continue awake. "Awake, thou that sleepest, and *Christ will give thee light*," is the call—inviting sinners to a point far beyond mere conviction. One who, for a whole year, went back to folly, said—"Your sermon on the corruption of the heart made me despair, and so I gave myself up to my old ways—attending dances, learning songs," &c. A knowledge of our guilt, and a sense of danger, will not of themselves keep us from falling; nay, these, if alone, may (as in the above case) thrust us down the slippery places. We are truly secure only when our eye is on Jesus, and our hand locked in his hand. So that the history of backslidings, instead of leading us to doubt the reality of grace in believers, will only be found to teach us two great lessons, viz., the vast importance of pressing immediate salvation on awakened souls, and the reasonableness of standing in doubt of all, however deep their convictions, who have not truly fled to the hope set before them.

There was another ground of prejudice against the whole work, arising from the circumstance that the Lord had employed in it young men not long engaged in the work of the ministry, rather than the fathers in Israel. But herein it was that sovereign grace shone forth the more conspicuously. Do such objectors suppose that God ever intends the honour of man in a work of Revival? Is it not the honour of his own name that he seeks? Had it been his wish to give the glory to man at all, then indeed it might have been asked, "Why does he pass by the older pastors, and call for the inexperienced youth?" But when sovereign grace was coming to bless a region in the way that would redound most to the glory of the Lord, can we conceive a wiser plan than to use the sling of David in bringing down the Philistine? If, however, there be some whose prejudice is from the root of envy, let such hear the remonstrance of Richard Baxter to the jealous ministers of his day. "What! malign Christ in gifts for which he should have the glory, and all because they seem to hinder our glory! Does not every man owe thanks to God for his brethren's gifts—not only as having himself part in them, as the foot has the benefit of the guidance of the eye, but also because his own ends may be attained by his brethren's gifts as well as by his own? . . . . . A fearful thing that any man, that hath the least of the fear of God, should so envy at God's gifts, that he would rather his carnal hearers were unconverted, and the drowsy not awakened, than that it should be done by another who may be preferred before them." [1]

The work of the Spirit went on, the stream flowing gently; for the heavy showers had fallen, and the overflowing of the waters had passed by. Mr M'Cheyne became more than ever vigilant and discriminating in dealing with souls. Observing, also, that some were influenced more by feelings of strong attachment to their pastor personally, than by the power of the truths he preached, he became more reserved in his dealings with them, so that some thought there was a little coldness or repulsiveness in his manner. If there did appear anything of this nature to some, certainly it was no indication of diminished compassion; but, on the contrary proceeded from a scrupulous anxiety to guard others against the deceitful feelings of their own souls. A few notes of his work occur at this period.

"November 27. 1839.—A pleasant meeting in the Cross Church on Wednesday last, for the seamen. All that spoke seemed to honour the Saviour. I had to move thanksgiving to God for his mercies. This has been a real blessing to Dundee. It should not be forgotten in our prayers and thanksgivings."

"Nov. 28—Thursday evening.—Much comfort in speaking. There was often an awful stillness. Spoke on Jerem. vi. 14—'They have healed also the hurt of the daughter of my people slightly,'" &c.

"December 1.—This evening came a tender Christian, so far as I can see; an exposition of that text, '*I will go softly,*' or of that other, '*Thou shalt not open thy mouth any more.*' A child of shame made one of honour. Her sister was awakened under Mr Baxter's words in St Peter's, of whom he asked, 'Would you like to be holy?' She replied, 'Indeed, I often wish I were dead that I might sin no more.'"

"Dec. 3.—Preached six times within these two days."

"Dec. 8.—Saw J. T. in fever. She seems really in Christ now; tells me how deeply my words sank into her soul when I was away. A. M. stayed to tell me her joy. J. B. walked home with me, telling me what God had done for his soul,

[1] *Reformed Pastor*, iv. 2.

144

when one day I had stopped at the quarry on account of a shower of rain, and took shelter with my pony in the engine-house." He had simply pointed to the fire of the furnace, and said, "What does that remind you of?" and the words had remained deep in the man's soul.

"Dec. 11.—A woman awakened that night I preached in J. D.'s green, about two years ago, on Ezek. xx. 43. For twenty years she had been out of Church privileges, and now, for the first time, came trembling to ask restoration. Surely Immanuel is in this place, and even old sinners are flocking to him. I have got an account of about twenty prayer-meetings connected with my flock. Many open ones; many fellowship meetings; only one or two have any thing like exhortation superadded to the Word. These, I think, it must be our care to change, if possible, lest error and pride creep in. The only other difficulty is this. In two of the female meetings, originally fellowship-meetings, anxious female inquirers have been admitted. They do not pray, but only hear. In one, M. and J. had felt the rising of pride to a great degree; in the other, M. could not be persuaded that there was any danger of pride. This case will require prayerful deliberation. My mind at present is, that there is great danger from it, the praying members feeling themselves on a different level from the others, and anything like female teaching, as a public teacher, seems clearly condemned in the Word of God."

"Dec. 12.—Felt very feeble all day, and as if I could not do any more work in the vineyard. Evening—Felt more of the reality of Immanuel's intercession. The people also were evidently subdued by more than a human testimony. One soul waited, sobbing most piteously. She could give no more account of herself than that she was a sinner, and did not believe that God would be merciful to her. When I showed how I found mercy, her only answer was—'But you were not sic a sinner as me.'"

"Dec. 18.—Went to Glasgow along with A. B. Preached in St George's to a full audience, in the cause of the Jews. Felt real help in time of need." This was one of his many journeys from place to place in behalf of Israel, relating the things seen and heard among the Jews of Palestine and other lands.

"Dec. 22.—Preached in Anderston Church, with a good deal of inward peace and comfort."

"Dec. 23.—Interesting meeting with the Jewish Committee. In the evening met a number of God's people. The horror of some good people in Glasgow at the Millenarian views is very great, while at the same time their objections appear very weak."

Dec. 31.—Young communicants. Two have made application to be admitted under eleven years of age; four that are only fourteen; three who are fifteen or sixteen."

"January 1. 1840.—Awoke early by the kind providence of God, and had uncommon freedom and fervency in keeping the concert for prayer this morning before light. Very touching interview with M. P., who still refuses to be comforted. Was enabled to cry after a glorious Immanuel along with her. How I wish I had her bitter convictions of sin! Another called this evening, who says she was awakened and brought to Christ during the sermon on the morning of December 1st, on the 'Covenant with death.' Gave clear answers, but seems too unmoved for one really changed."

"Jan. 2.—Visited six families. Was refreshed and solemnized at each of them. Spoke of the Word made flesh, and of all the paths of the Lord being mercy and truth. Visited in the evening by some interesting souls: one a believing little boy; another complaining she cannot come to Christ for the hardness of her heart; another once awakened under my ministry, again thoroughly awakened and brought to Christ under Horace Bonar's sermon at the Communion. She is the only saved one in her family—awfully persecuted by father and mother. Lord, stand up for thine own! Make known by their constancy under suffering, the power and beauty of thy grace! Evening—Mr Miller preached delightfully on 'The love of Christ constraineth us.' His account of the Protestants of France was very interesting—the work of God at Nismes, where it is said they are no more fishing with line, but dragging with the nets. Read a letter from Mr Cumming, describing the work at Perth, and entreating the prayers of God's children."

This last reference is to the awakening which took place in St Leonard's Church, Perth, on the last night of the year, when Mr Burns, along with their pastor, Mr Milne, was preaching. Mr B. had intended to return to Dundee for the Sabbath, but was detained by the plain indications of the Lord's presence. At one meeting, the work was so glorious that one night about 150 persons at one time seemed bowed down under a sense of their guilt, and above 200 came next day to the church in the forenoon to converse about their souls. This awakening was the commencement of a solid work of grace, both in that town and its neighbourhood, much fruit of which is to be found there at this day in souls that are walking in the fear of the Lord, and the comfort of the Holy Ghost. And it was in the spring of this same year, that, in Collace, at our weekly prayer-meeting, when two brethren were ministering, we received a blessed shower from the Lord.

His Journal proceeds:—

"Jan. 3.—An inquirer came, awakened under my ministry two years and a half ago."

"Jan. 5.—Two came; M. B. sorely wounded with the forenoon's discourse."

"Jan. 12.—Intimated a concert for prayer, that unworthy communicants might be kept back, the Lord's children prepared for the feast, and ministers furnished from on high."

"Jan. 13.—Kept concert of prayer this morning with my dear people. Did not find the same enlargement as usual."

"March 5—Thursday evening.—Preached on Zech. iii.—Joshua. Was led to speak searchingly about making Christ the minister of sin. One young woman cried aloud very bitterly. M. B. came to tell me that poor M. is like to have her life taken away by her parents. A young woman also, who is still concerned, and persecuted by her father. A young man came to tell me that he had found Christ. Roll on, thou river of life! visit every dwelling! save a multitude of souls. Come, Holy Spirit! come quickly!"

"March 25.—Last night at Forfar speaking for Israel to

a small band of friends of the Jews. Fearfully wicked place —the cry of it ascends up before God like that of Sodom."

"March 31.—Met with young communicants on Wednesday and Friday. On the latter night especially, very deep feeling, manifested in sobbings. Visits of several. One dear child nine years old. Sick bed."

"April 1.—Presbytery day. Passed the constitution of two new churches—blessed be God!—may he raise up faithful pastors for them both—Dudhope and Wallace-Feus. Proposal also for the Mariners' Church. A fast-day fixed for the present state of the Church."

"April 5. Sabbath evening.—Spoke to twenty-four young persons, one by one; almost all affected about their souls."

"April 6.—Lovely ride and meditation in a retired grove."

"April 7.—Impressed to-night with the complete necessity of preaching to my people in their own lanes and closes; in no other way will God's Word ever reach them. To-night spoke in St Andrew's Church to a very crowded assembly in behalf of Israel. Was helped to speak plainly to their own consciences. Lord bless it! Shake this town!"

"April 13.—Spoke in private to nearly thirty young communicants, all in one room, going round each, and advising for the benefit of all."

"April 22.—Rode to Collessie (Fife) and Kirkaldy. Sweet time alone in Collessie woods."

"July 30.—One lad came to me in great distress wishing to know if he should confess his little dishonesties to his master." About this time, he has noted down, "I was visiting the other day, and came to a locked door. What did this mean? 'Torment me not, torment me not.' Ah, Satan is mighty still"—referring to Mark v. 7.

A few of his Communion seasons are recorded. We could have desired a record of them all. The first of which he has detailed any particulars, is the one he enjoyed soon after returning home.

"January 19. 1840.—Stormy morning, with gushing torrents of rain, but cleared up in answer to prayer. Sweet union in prayer with Mr Cumming, and afterwards with A. Bonar. Found God in secret. Asked especially that the very sight of the broken bread and poured-out wine might be blessed to some souls, then pride will be hidden from man. Church well filled—many standing. Preached the action sermon on John xvii. 24, 'Father I will,' &c. Had considerable nearness to God in prayer—more than usual—and also freedom in preaching, although I was ashamed of such poor views of Christ's glory. The people were in a very desirable frame of attention—hanging on the word. Felt great help in fencing the tables, from Acts v. 3, 'Lying to the Holy Ghost.' Came down and served the first table, with much more calmness and collectedness than ever I remember to have enjoyed. Enjoyed a sweet season while A. B. served the next table. He dwelt chiefly on believing the words of Christ about his fullness, and the promise of the Father. There were six tables altogether. The people more and more moved to the end. At the last table, every head seemed bent like a bulrush while A. B. spoke of the ascension of Christ. Helped a little in the address, 'Now to him who is able to keep you,' &c., and in the concluding prayer. One little boy, in retiring, said, 'This has been another bonnie day.' Many of the little ones seemed deeply attentive. Mr Cumming and Mr Burns preached in the school the most of the day. In the evening Mr C. preached on the Pillar Cloud on every dwelling, Isaiah iv. 5, some very sweet, powerful words. Mr Burns preached in the school-room. When the church emptied, a congregation formed in the lower school, and began to sing. Sang several psalms with them, and spoke on 'Behold, I stand at the door.' Going home, A. L. said, 'Pray for me; I am quite happy, and so is H.' Altogether a day of the revelation of Christ—a sweet day to myself, and, I am persuaded, to many souls. Lord, make us meet for the table above."

Another of these Communion seasons recorded, is April 1840. "Sabbath 19.—Sweet and precious day. Preached action sermon on Zech. xii. 10; xiii. 1. A good deal assisted. Also in fencing the tables, on Psa. cxxxix., 'Search me, O God.' Less at serving the tables, on 'I will betroth thee,' and 'To him that overcometh;' though the thanksgiving was sweet. Communicated with calm joy. Old Mr Burns served two tables; H. Bonar five. There was a very melting frame visible among the people. Helped a good deal in the address on 'My sheep hear my voice.' After seven before all was over. Met before eight. Old Mr Burns preached on 'A word in season.' Gave three parting texts, and so concluded this blessed day. Many were filled with joy unspeakable and full of glory."

"Monday 20.—Mr Grierson preached on, 'Ye are come to Mount Zion'—an instructive word. Pleasant walk with H. B. Evening sermon from him to the little children on the 'new heart'—truly delightful. Prayer-meeting after. I began ; then old Mr Burns; then Horace, in a very lively manner, on the 'woman of Samaria.' The people were brought into a very tender frame. After the blessing, a multitude remained. One (A. N.) was like a person struck through with a dart; she could neither stand nor go. Many were looking on her with faces of horror. Others were comforting her in a very kind manner, bidding her look to Jesus. Mr Burns went to the desk, and told them of Kilsyth. Still they would not go away. Spoke a few words more to those around me, telling them of the loveliness of Christ, and the hardness of their hearts, that they could be so unmoved when one was so deeply wounded. The sobbing soon spread, till many heads were bent down, and the church was filled with sobbing. Many whom I did not know were now affected. After prayer, we dismissed, near midnight. Many followed us. One, in great agony, prayed that she might find Christ that very night. So ends this blessed season."

The prayer-meeting on the Monday evening following the Communion was generally enjoyed by all the Lord's people, and by the ministers who assisted, in a peculiar manner. Often all felt the last day of the feast to be the great day. Souls that had been enjoying the feast were then, at its conclusion, taking hold on the arm of the Beloved in the prospect of going up through the wilderness.

The only notice of his last Communion, January 1, 1843, is the following.—"Sabbath—A happy Communion season. Mr W. Burns preached on Tuesday, Wednesday, and Thursday evenings—the first and last very solemn. Mr Baxter (of Hilltown Church) on the Friday. A. Bonar on Saturday, on

Rom. viii.—the spirit of adoption. I fainted on the Sabbath morning, but revived, and got grace and strength to preach on 1 Tim. i. 16—Paul's conversion a pattern. There were five tables. Many godly strangers, and a very desirable frame observable in the people. 'While the king sitteth at his table, my spikenard sendeth out the smell thereof.' Much sin was covered. He restoreth my soul. Monday 2.—Mr Milne (of Perth) preached on, 'Hold fast that thou hast;' and in the evening, to the children, on Josh. xxiv. 'Choose ye this day whom ye will serve.' Andrew and I concluded with Rev. v. 'Thou has redeemed us,' &c., and I Cor. xv. 'Be stedfast,' &c."

He dispensed the Lord's Supper to his flock every quarter; and though on this account his calls upon his brethren for help were frequent, yet never did a brother reckon it anything else than a blessed privilege to be with him. His first invitation to his friend Mr Hamilton (then at Abernyte), will show the nature of the intercourse that subsisted between him and his brethren who gave their services on these occasions:—"My dear friend, Will you excuse lack of ceremony, and come down to-morrow and preach to us the unsearchable riches of Christ? We have the Communion on Sabbath. We have no fast-day, but only a meeting in the evening at a quarter past seven. Come, my dear Sir, if you can, and refresh us with your company. Bring the fragrance of 'the bundle of myrrh' along with you, and may grace be poured into your lips. Yours ever." (Jan. 15. 1840.)

Soon after his return from his Mission to the Jews, a ministerial prayer-meeting was formed among some of the brethren in Dundee. Mr M'Cheyne took part in it, along with Mr Lewis of St David's, Mr Baxter of Hilltown, Mr P. L. Miller, afterwards of Wallacetown, and others. Feeling deep concern for the salvation of the souls under their care, they met every Monday forenoon, to pray together for their flocks, and their own souls. The time of the meeting was limited to an hour and a half, in order that all who attended might form their pastoral arrangements for the day, without fear of being hindered; and, in addition to prayer, those present conversed on some selected topic, vitally connected with their duties as ministers of Christ. Mr M'Cheyne was never absent from this prayer-meeting, unless through absolute necessity, and the brethren scarcely remember any occasion on which some important remark did not drop from his lips. He himself reaped great profit from it. He notes, December 8th—"This has been a deeply interesting week. On Monday our ministerial prayer-meeting was set agoing in St David's vestry. The hearts of all seem really in earnest in it. The Lord answers prayer; may it be a great blessing to our souls and to our flocks." Another time—"Meeting in St David's vestry. The subject of fasting was spoken upon. Felt exceedingly in my own spirit how little we feel real grief on account of sin before God, or we would often lose our appetite for food. When parents lose a child, they often do not taste a bit from morning to night, out of pure grief. Should we not mourn as for an only child? How little of the spirit of grace and supplication we have then!" On Dec. 30—"Pleasant meeting of ministers. Many delightful texts on 'Arguments to be used with God in prayer.' How little I have used these! Should we not study prayer more?"

Full as he was of affection and Christian kindness to all believers, he was specially so to the faithful brethren in the gospel of Christ. Perhaps there never was one who more carefully watched against the danger of undervaluing precious men, and detracting from a brother's character. Although naturally ambitious, grace so wrought in him, that he never sought to bring himself into view; and most cheerfully would he observe and take notice of the graces and gifts of others. Who is there of us that should ever feel otherwise? "For the body is not one member, but many," And "the eye cannot say unto the hand, I have no need of thee; nor, again, the head to the feet, I have no need of you."

All with whom he was intimate still remember with gratitude how faithfully and anxiously he used to warn his friends of whatever he apprehended they were in danger from. To Mr W. C. Burns he wrote, Dec. 31, 1839: "Now, the Lord be your strength, teacher, and guide. I charge you, be clothed with humility, or you will yet be a wandering star, for which is reserved the blackness of darkness for ever. Let Christ increase; let man decrease. This is my constant prayer for myself and you. If you lead sinners to yourself, and not to Christ, Immanuel will cast the star out of his right hand into utter darkness. Remember what I said of preaching out of the Scriptures; honour the Word both in the matter and manner. Do not cease to pray for me." At another time (Nov. 3. 1841), he thus wrote to the same friend : "Now, remember Moses wist not that the skin of his face shone. Looking at our own shining face is the bane of the spiritual life and of the ministry. O for closest communion with God, till soul and body—head, face, and heart—shine with divine brilliancy; but O for a holy ignorance of our shining. Pray for this; for you need it as well as I."

To another friend in the ministry who had written to him despondingly about his people and the times, his reply was, "I am sure there never was a time when the Spirit of God was more present in Scotland, and it does not become you to murmur in your tents, but rather to give thanks. Remember, we may grieve the Spirit as truly by not joyfully acknowledging his wonders as by not praying for him. There is the clearest evidence that God is saving souls in Kilsyth, Dundee, Perth, Collace, Blairgowrie, Strathbogie, Ross-shire, Breadalbane, Kelso, Jedburgh, Ancrum; and surely it becomes us to say, "I thank my God upon every remembrance of you.' Forgive my presumption; but I fear lest you hurt your own peace and usefulness in not praising God enough for the operation of his hands." To another: "I have told you that you needed trial, and now it is come. May you be exercised thereby, and come to that happy 'afterwards' of which the Apostle speaks." To the same again : "Remember the necessity of your own soul, and do not grow slack or lean in feeding others. 'Mine own vineyard have I not kept.' Ah, take heed of that !" And in a similar tone of faithfulness at an after period : 'Remember the case of your own soul. 'What will it profit a man to gain the whole world and lose his own soul?' Remember how often Paul appeals to his holy, just, unblameable life. O that we may be able always to do the same !" "Remember the pruning-knife," he says to another, "and do not let your vine run to wood." And after a visit to Mr Thornton of Milnathort, in whose parish there had been an awakening, he asks a brother, "Mr Thornton is willing that others be blessed more than himself; do you think that you have that grace? I find that I am never so successful as when I can lie at Christ's feet, willing to be used or not as seemeth good in his sight. Do you remember David? 'If the Lord say I have no delight in thee; behold, here am I; let him do to me as seemeth good unto him.'" In his familiar letters, as in his life, there was the manifestation of a bright, cheerful soul, without the least tendency to levity. When his medical attendant had, on one occasion, declined any remuneration, Mr M'Cheyne peremptorily opposed his purpose; and to overcome his reluctance, returned the inclosure in a letter, in which he used his poetical gifts with most pleasant humour.

To many it was a subject of wonder that he found time to write letters that always breathed the name of Jesus, amid his innumerable engagements. But the truth was, his letters cost him no expenditure of time; they were ever the fresh thoughts and feelings of his soul at the moment he took up the pen; his habitual frame of soul is what appears in them all. The calm, holy, tenderly-affectionate style of his letters reminds us of Samuel Rutherford, whose works he delighted to read—excepting only that his joy never seems to have risen to ecstasies. The selection of his letters which I have made for publication, may exhibit somewhat of his holy skill in dropping a word for his Master on all occasions. But what impressed many yet more, was his manner of introducing the truth, most naturally and strikingly, even in the shortest note he penned; and there was something so elegant, as well as solemn, in his few words at the close of some of his letters, that these remained deep in the receiver's heart. Writing to Mr G. S. on July 28, 1841, he thus draws to a close: "Remember me to H. T. I pray he may be kept abiding in Christ. Kindest regards to his mother. Say to her from me, 'Pass the time of your sojourning here in fear, forasmuch as ye know ye were not redeemed with corruptible things such as silver and gold;' 1 Peter i. 17, 18. Keep your own heart, dear brother, 'in the love of God' (Jude 21), in his love to you, and that will draw your love to him. Kindest remembrances to your brother. Say to him, 'Be sober and hope to the end.' (1 Peter i. 13). To your own dear mother say, 'He doth not afflict willingly.' Write me soon.—Ever yours, till time shall be no more." In a note to the members of his own family:—"The Tay is before me now like a resplendent mirror, glistening in the morning sun. May the same sun shine sweetly on you, and may He that makes it shine, shine into your hearts to give you the knowledge of the glory of God in the face of Jesus Christ.—In haste, your affectionate son and brother." There were often such last words as the following—"O for drops in the pastures of the wilderness! The smiles of Jesus be with you, and the breathings of the Holy Ghost. Ever yours." (To Rev. J. Milne.) "May we have gales passing from Perth to this, and from here to you, and from heaven to both. Ever yours." (To the same.) "The time is short; eternity is near; yea, the coming of Christ the second time is at hand. Make sure of being one with the Lord Jesus, that you may be glad when you see him. Commending you all to our Father in heaven," &c. (To his own brother.) "I have a host of letters before me, and therefore can add no more. I give you a parting text, 'Sorrowful, yet always rejoicing." Another—"Farewell! yours till the day dawn." To the Rev. Hor. Bonar he says, at the close of a letter about some ministerial arrangements, "I am humbled and cheered by what you say of good done in Kelso. Roll on, roll on, river of God, that art full of water. A woman came to me, awakened under your sermon to the children in the Cross Church, very bitterly convinced of sin. Glory to the Divine Archer, who bringeth down the people!" He closes a letter to a student thus: "Grace be with you, and much of the knowledge of Jesus—much of his likeness. I thirst for the knowledge of the Word, but most of all of Jesus himself, the True Word. May he abide in you, and you in him! The fear of Isaac watch over you." In concluding a letter to Mr Bonar of Larbert, in February 1843, some weeks before his last illness, he writes—"My soul often goes out at the throne of grace in behalf of Larbert and Dunipace. May the disruption be more blessed to them than days of peace! How sweet to be in the ark when the deluge comes down. Ever yours in gospel bonds."

The Jewish Mission continued near his heart, " the nearest," said he to Mr Edwards, who is now at Jassy, "of all missionary enterprises. Were it not for my own unfitness, and also the success the Lord has given me where I am, I would joyfully devote myself to it." In connection with this cause, he was invited to visit Ireland, and be present at the meeting of the Synod of our Presbyterian brethren in the summer of 1840. When preparing to set out, he notices the hand of his Master guiding him :—"July 2.—Expected to have been in Ireland this day. Detained by not being able to get supply for Sabbath, in the good providence of God, for this evening there was a considerable awakening in the Church while I was preaching upon Philip. iii. 18, 'Enemies of the cross of Christ.' When that part was expounded there was a loud and bitter weeping—probably thirty or forty seemed to share in it; the rest deeply impressed—many secretly praying." On the Sabbath following, one person was so overcome as to be carried out of the church.

He set out for Ireland on the 7th, and on the 10th witnessed at Belfast the union between the Synod of Ulster and the Secession. He speaks of it as a most solemn scene—500 ministers and elders present. During his stay there, he pleaded the cause of the Jews in Mr Morgan's church, Mr Wilson's, and some others; and also visited Mr Kirkpatrick at Dublin. He preached the way of salvation to the Gentiles in all his pleadings for Israel. His visit was blessed to awaken a deep interest in the cause of the Jews, and his words sank into the consciences of some. His sermon on Ezekiel xxxiv. 16, was felt by some to be indescribably impressive; and when he preached on Rom. i. 16, 17, many ministers, as they came out, were heard saying, "How was it we never thought of the duty of remembering Israel before?" On another occasion, the people to whom he had preached entreated their minister to try and get him again, and if he could not preach to them, that at least he should pray once more with them.

He was not, however, long absent from home on this occasion. On the 25th, I find him recording—"Reached home; entirely unprepared for the evening. Spoke on Psalm li. 12, 13, 'Restore unto me the joy,' &c. There seemed much of the presence of God—first one crying out in extreme agony, then another. Many were deeply melted, and all solemnized. Felt a good deal of freedom in speaking of the glory of Christ's salvation. Coming down, I spoke quietly to some whom I knew to be under deep concern. They were soon heard together, weeping bitterly; many more joined them. Mr Cumming spoke to them in a most touching strain, while I dealt privately with several in the vestry. Their cries were often very bitter and piercing, bitterest when the freeness of Christ was pressed upon them, and the lion's nearness. Several were offended; but I felt no hesitation as to our duty to declare the simple truth impressively, and leave God to work in their hearts in his own way. If he save souls in a quiet way I shall be happy; if in the midst of cries and tears, still I will bless his name. One painful thing has occurred: a man who pretends to be a missionary for Israel, and who brings forward the Apocryphal book of Enoch, has been among my people, in my absence, and many have been led after him. How humbling is this to them and to me! Lord, what is man! This may be blessed, 1st, to discover chaff which we thought to be wheat; 2nd, To lead some to greater distrust of themselves, when their eyes are opened; 3rd, To teach me the need of solidly instructing those who seem to have grace in their hearts."

The work of God went on, so much so at this time, that he gave it as his belief, in a letter to Mr Purves of Jedburgh, that for some months about this period no minister of Christ had preached in a lively manner, without being blessed to some soul among his flock.

In other places of Scotland also the Lord was then pouring out his Spirit. Perth has been already mentioned, and its vicinity. Throughout Ross-shire, whole congregations were frequently moved as one man, and the voice of the minister drowned in the cries of anxious souls. At Kelso, where Mr Horace Bonar laboured, and at Jedburgh, where

Mr Purves was pastor, a more silent, but very solid work of conversion was advancing. At Ancrum (once the scene of John Livingston's labours), the whole parish, but especially the men of the place, were awakened to the most solemn concern. On Lochtayside, where Mr Burns was for a season labouring, there were marks of the Spirit everywhere; and the people crossing the lake in hundreds, to listen to the words of life on the hill-side, called to mind the people of Galilee in the days when the Gospel began to be preached. At Lawers, Mr Campbell, their pastor (who has now fallen asleep in Jesus), spoke of the awakening as "like a resurrection," so great and sudden was the change from deadness to intense concern. On several occasions, the Spirit seemed to sweep over the congregations like wind over the fields, which bends the heavy corn to the earth. It was evident to discerning minds, that the Lord was preparing Scotland for some crisis not far distant.

Several districts of Strathbogie had shared to some extent in a similar blessing. Faithful ministers were now everywhere on the watch for the shower, and were greatly strengthened to go forward boldly in seeking to cleanse the sanctuary. It was their fond hope that the Established Church of Scotland would soon become an example and pattern to the nations of a pure Church of Christ, acknowledged and upheld by the State, without being trammelled in any degree, far less controlled by civil interference. But Satan was stirring up adversaries on every side.

The Court of Session had adopted a line of procedure that was at once arbitrary and unconstitutional. And now that Court interdicted, under the penalty of fine or imprisonment, all the ministers of the Church of Scotland from administering ordinances or preaching the Word in any of the seven parishes of Strathbogie, whose former incumbents had been suspended from office by the General Assembly for ecclesiastical offences. The Church saw it to be her duty to refuse obedience to an interdict, which hindered the preaching of Jesus, and attempted to crush her constitutional liberties. Accordingly, ministers were sent to these districts, fearless of the result; and under their preaching the gross darkness of the region began to give way to the light of truth.

In the month of August, Mr M'Cheyne was appointed, along with Mr Cumming of Dumbarney, to visit Huntly, and dispense the Lord's Supper there. As he set out he expressed the hope, that "the dews of the Spirit there might be turned into the pouring rain." His own visit was blessed to many. Mr Cumming preached the action sermon in the open air at the Meadow Well; but the tables were served within the building where the congregation usually met. Mr M'Cheyne preached in the evening to a vast multitude at the well; and about a hundred waited after sermon for prayer, many of them in deep anxiety.

He came to Edinburgh on the 11th, to attend the meeting of ministers and elders who had come together to sign the *Solemn Engagement* in defence of the liberties of Christ's Church. He hesitated not to put his hand to the Engagement. He then returned to Dundee; and scarcely had he returned, when he was laid aside by one of those attacks of illness with which he was so often tried. In this case, however, it soon passed away. "My health," he remarked, "has taken a gracious turn, which should make me look up." But again, on September 6th, an attack of fever laid him down for six days. On this occasion, just before the sickness came on, three persons had visited him, to tell him how they were brought to Christ under his ministry some years before. "Why," he noted in his journal, "Why has God brought these cases before me *this week*? Surely he is preparing me for some trial of faith." The result proved that his conjecture was just. And while his Master prepared him beforehand for these trials, he had ends to accomplish in his servant by means of them. There were other trials also, besides these, which were very heavy to him; but in all we could discern the husbandman pruning the branch, that it might bear more fruit. As he himself said one day in the church of Abernyte, when he was assisting Mr Manson, "If we only saw the whole, we should see that the Father is doing little else in the world but *training his vines*."

His preaching became more and more to him a work of

faith. Often I find him writing at the close or beginning of a sermon:—"Master, help," "Help, Lord, help," "Send showers," "Pardon, give the Spirit, and take the glory," "May the opening of my lips be right things." The piercing effects of the word preached on souls at this season may be judged of, from what one of the awakened, with whom he was conversing, said to him, *I think hell would be some relief from an angry God.*"

His delight in preaching was very great. He himself used to say that he could scarcely ever resist an invitation to preach. And this did not arise from the natural excitement there is in commanding the attention of thousands; for he was equally ready to proclaim Christ to small country flocks. Nay, he was ready to travel far to visit and comfort even one soul. There was an occasion this year on which he rode far to give a cup of cold water to a disciple, and his remark was, "I observe how often Jesus went a long way for one soul, as for example the maniac, and the woman of Canaan."

In February 1841, he visited Kelso and Jedburgh at the communion season; and gladly complied with an invitation to Ancrum also, that he might witness the hand of the Lord. "Sweet are the spots," he wrote, "where Immanuel has ever shown his glorious power in the conviction and conversion of sinners. The world loves to muse on the scenes where battles were fought and victories won. Should not we love the spots where our great Captain has won his amazing victories? Is not the conversion of a soul more worthy to be spoken of than the taking of Acre?" At Kelso, some will long remember his remarks in visiting a little girl, to whom he said, "Christ gives last knocks. When your heart becomes hard and careless, then fear lest Christ may have given a *last knock.*" At Jedburgh, the impression left was chiefly that there had been among them a man of peculiar holiness. Some felt, not so much his words, as his presence and holy solemnity, as if one spoke to them who was standing in the presence of God; and to others his prayers appeared like the breathings of one already within the veil.

I find him proposing to a minister who was going up to the General Assembly that year, "that the Assembly should draw out a *Confession of Sin*, for all its ministers." The state, also, of parishes under the direful influence of Moderatism, lay much upon his spirit. In his diary he writes—"Have been laying much to heart the absolute necessity laid upon the Church of sending the gospel to our dead parishes, during the life of the present incumbents. It is confessed that many of our ministers do not preach the gospel—alas! because they know it not. Yet they have complete control over their own pulpits, and may never suffer the truth to be heard there during their whole incumbency. And yet our Church consigns these parishes to their tender mercies for perhaps fifty years, without a sigh! Should not certain men be ordained as Evangelists, with full power to preach in every pulpit of their district—faithful, judicious, lively preachers, who may go from parish to parish, and thus carry life into many a dead corner?" This was a subject he often reverted to; and he eagerly held up the example of the Presbytery of Aberdeen, who made a proposal to this effect. From some of his later letters, it appears that he had sometimes seriously weighed the duty of giving up his fixed charge, if only the Church would ordain him as an Evangelist. So deep were his feelings on this matter, that a friend relates of him, that as they rode together through a parish where the pastor "clothed himself with the wool, but fed not the flock," he knit his brow and raised his hand with vehemence as he spoke of the people left to perish under such a minister.

He was invited to visit Ireland again this year, his former visit having been much valued by the Presbyterian brethren there. He did so in July. Many were greatly stirred up by his preaching, and by his details of God's work in Scotland. His sermon on Song viii. 5, 6, is still spoken of by many. His prayerfulness and consistent holiness left enduring impressions on not a few; and it was during his visit that a memorial was presented to the Irish Assembly in behalf of a Jewish mission. His visit was in a great measure the means of setting that mission on foot.

Cordially entering into the proposal of the concert for prayer, he took part, in September of this year, in the preliminary meetings in which Christians of all denominations joined. "How sweet are the smallest approximations to unity," is his remark in his diary. Indeed, he so much longed for a scriptural unity, that some time after, when the General Assembly had repealed the statute of 1799, he embraced the opportunity of showing his sincere desire for unity, by inviting two dissenting brethren to his pulpit, and then writing in defence of his conduct when attacked. In reference to this matter, he observed, in a note to a friend—"I have been much delighted with the 25th and 26th chapters of the Confession of Faith. O for the grace of the Westminster divines to be poured out upon this generation of lesser men!"

As it was evident that his Master owned his labour abundantly, by giving him seals of his apostleship, there were attempts made occasionally by zealous friends to induce him to remove to other spheres. In all these cases, he looked simply at the apparent indications of the Lord's will. Worldly interest seemed scarcely ever to cross his mind in regard to such a matter, for he truly lived a disinterested life. His views may be judged of by one instance—a letter to Mr Heriot of Ramornie, in reference to a charge which many were anxious to offer him.

"DUNDEE, 24th December, 1841.

"DEAR SIR,—I have received a letter from my friend Mr M'Farlane of Collessie, asking what I would do if the people of Kettle were to write desiring me to be their minister. He also desires me to send an answer to you. I have been asked to leave this place again and again, but have never seen my way clear to do so. I feel quite at the disposal of my Divine Master. I gave myself away to him when I began my ministry, and he has guided me as by the Pillar Cloud from the first day till now. I think I would leave this place to-morrow if he were to *bid* me; but as to *seeking removal*, I dare *not* and *could not*. If my ministry were unsuccessful —if God frowned upon the place and made my message void —then I would willingly go; for I would rather beg my bread than preach without success; but I have never wanted success. I do not think I can speak a month in this parish without winning some souls. This very week I think has been a fruitful one, more so than many for a long time, which perhaps was intended graciously to free me from all hesitation in declining your kind offer. I mention these things, not, I trust, boastfully, but only to show you the ground upon which I feel it to be my duty not for a moment to entertain the proposal. I have 4000 souls here hanging on me. I have as much of this world's goods as I care for. I have full liberty to preach the Gospel night and day; and the Spirit of God is often with us. What can I desire more? 'I dwell among mine own people.' Hundreds look to me as a father; and I fear I would be but a false shepherd if I were to leave them when the clouds of adversity are beginning to lower. I know the need of Kettle, and its importance; and also the dark prospect of your getting a godly minister. Still that is a future event in the hand of God. My duty is made plain and simple according to God's Word.

"Praying that the Lord Jesus may send you a star from his own right hand, believe me to be," &c.

It was during this year that the Sabbath question began to interest him so much. His tract "I love the Lord's Day," was published December 18th; but he had already exerted himself much in this cause, as Convener of the Committee of Presbytery on Sabbath Observance, and had written his well-known letter to one of the chief defenders of the Sabbath desecration. He continued unceasingly to use every effort in this holy cause. And is it not worth the prayers and self-denying efforts of every believing man? Is not that day set apart as a season wherein the Lord desires the refreshing rest of his own love to be offered to a fallen world? Is it not designed to be a day on which every other voice and sound is to be hushed, in order that the silver trumpets may proclaim atonement for sinners? Nay, it is understood to be a day wherein God himself stands before the altar and pleads with sinners to accept the Lamb slain, from morning to evening! Who is there that does not see the deep design of Satan in seeking to effect an inroad on this most merciful appointment of God our Saviour?

Mr M'Cheyne's own conduct was in full accordance with

his principles in regard to strict yet cheerful Sabbath observance. Considering it the summit of human privilege to be
admitted to fellowship with God, his principle was, that the
Lord's Day was to be spent wholly in the enjoyment of that
sweetest privilege. A letter, written at a later period, but
bearing on this subject, will show how he felt this day to be
better than a thousand. An individual near Inverness had
consulted him on a point of Sabbatical casuistry : the question was, Whether or not it was sinful to spend time in regis-
tering meteorological observations on the Sabbaths? His
reply was the following, marked by a holy wisdom, and discovering the place which the Lord held in his inmost soul :—

"*December* 7, 1842.

"DEAR FRIEND,—You ask me a hard question. Had you
asked me *what I would do in the case*, I could easily tell you.
I love the Lord's Day too well to be marking down the
height of the thermometer and barometer every hour. I
have other work to do, higher and better, and more like that
of angels above. The more entirely I can give my Sabbaths
to God, and half forget that I am not before the throne of
the Lamb, with my harp of gold, the happier am I, and I
feel it my duty to be as happy as I can be, and as God intended me to be. The joy of the Lord is my strength. But
whether another Christian can spend the Sabbath in his service, and mark down degrees of heat and atmospherical pres-
sure, without letting down the warmth of his affections, or
losing the atmosphere of heaven, I cannot tell. My conscience
is not the rule of another man. One thing we may learn
from these men of science, namely, to be as careful in marking the changes and progress of our own spirit, as they are in
marking the changes of the weather. An hour should never
pass without our looking up to God for forgiveness and
peace. This is the noblest science, to know how to live in
hourly communion with God in Christ. May you and I
know more of this, and thank God that we are not among
the wise and prudent from whom these things are hid !—The
grace of the Lord of the Sabbath be with you," &c.

Up till this period, the *Narrative of our Mission to Israel* had not been given to the public. Interruptions, arising from multiplicity of labours and constant calls of duty, had from time to time come in our way. Mr M'Cheyne found it exceedingly difficult to spare a day or two at a time in order to take part. "I find it hard work to carry on the work of a diligent pastor and that of an author at the same time. How John Calvin would have smiled at my difficulties!" At length, however, in the month of March 1842, we resolved to gain time by exchanging each other's pastoral duties for a month. Accordingly, during four or five weeks, he remained in Collace, my flock enjoying his Sabbath-day services and his occasional visits, while he was set free from what would have been the never-ceasing interruptions of his own town.

Many a pleasant remembrance remains of these days, as sheet after sheet passed under the eyes of our mutual criticism. Though intent on accomplishing his work, he kept by his rule, "that he must first see the face of God before he could undertake any duty." Often would he wander in the mornings among the pleasant woods of Dunsinnan, till he had drunk in refreshment to his soul by meditation on the Word of God; and then he took up the pen. And to a brother in the ministry, who had one day broken in upon his close occupation, he afterwards wrote—"You know you stole away my day; yet I trust all was not lost. I think I have had more grace ever since that prayer among the fir-trees. O to be *like* Jesus, and *with* him to all eternity." Occasionally, during the same period, he wrote some pieces for the "Christian's Daily Companion." The Narrative was finished in May, and the Lord has made it acceptable to the brethren.

When this work was finished, the Lord had other employment ready for him in his own parish. His diary has this entry: "May 22nd—I have seen some very evident awakenings of late. J. G. awakened partly through the Word preached, and partly through the faithful warnings of her fellow-servant. A. R., who has been for about a year in the deepest distress, seeking rest, but finding none. B. M. converted last winter at the Tuesday meeting in Annfield. She was brought very rapidly to peace with God, and to a calm, sedate, prayerful state of mind. I was surprised at the quickness of the work in this case, and pleased with the clear tokens of grace; and now I see God's gracious end in it. She was to be admitted at last communion, but caught fever before the Sabbath. On Tuesday last, she died in great peace and joy. When she felt death coming on, she said, 'O death, death, come! let us sing!' Many that knew her have been a good deal moved homeward by this solemn providence. This evening, I invited those to come who are leaving the parish at this term. About twenty came, to whom I gave tracts and words of warning. *I feel persuaded that if I could follow the Lord more fully myself, my ministry would be used to make a deeper impression than it has yet done.*"

CHAPTER VI

THE LATTER DAYS OF HIS MINISTRY

"My meat is to do the will of him that sent me, and to finish his work."—JOHN iv. 34.

DURING the summer of 1842, he was exposed to several attacks of illness, experienced some severe personal trials, and felt the assaults of sore temptation. His own words will best express his state. "July 17th—I am myself much tempted, and have no hope, but as a worm on the arm of Jesus." "August 4th—Often, often, would I have been glad to depart, and be with Christ. I am now much better in body and mind, having a little of the presence of my Beloved whose absence is death to me." The same month—"I have been carried through deep waters, bodily and spiritual, since last we met." It was his own persuasion that few had more to struggle with in the inner man. Who can tell what wars go on within?

During this season of trial, he was invited to form one of a number of ministers from Scotland, who were to visit the north of England, with no other purpose than to preach the glad tidings. The scheme was planned by a Christian gentleman, who has done much for Christ in his generation. When the invitation reached him, he was in the heat of his furnace. He mentioned this to the brother who corresponded with him on the subject, Mr Purves of Jedburgh, whose reply was balm to his spirit. . . . "I have a fellow-feeling with you in your present infirmity, and you know for your consolation that another has, who is a brother indeed. In all our afflictions, he is afflicted. He is, we may say, the common heart of his people; for they are one body, and an infirmity in the very remotest and meanest member is felt *there* and borne *there*. Let us console, solace, yea, satiate ourselves in him, as, amid afflictions especially, brother does in brother. It is blessed to be like him in everything, even in suffering. There is a great want about all Christians who have not suffered. Some flowers must be broken or bruised before they emit any fragrance. All the wounds of Christ send out sweetness —all the sorrows of Christians do the same. Commend me to a bruised brother, a broken reed—one like the Son of Man. The Man of Sorrows is never far from him. To me there is something sacred and sweet in all suffering; it is so much akin to the Man of Sorrows." It was thus he suffered, and thus that he was comforted. He wrote back, agreeing to go, and added, "Remember me especially, who am heavy laden oftentimes. My heart is all of sin; but Jesus lives."

They set out for England. Mr Purves, Mr Somerville of Anderston, Mr Cumming of Dumbarney, and Mr Bonar of Kelso, formed the company. Their chief station was Newcastle, where Mr Burns had been recently labouring with some success, and where he had seen "a town giving itself up to utter ungodliness—a town where Satan's trenches were deep and wide, his wall strong and high, his garrison great and fearless, and where all that man could do seemed but as arrows shot against a tower of brass." But those who went knew that the Spirit of God was omnipotent, and that he could take the prey from the mighty.

They preached both in the open air and in the places of worship belonging to the Presbyterians and to the Wesleyan

Methodists. The defenders of the Sabbath cause were specially prepared to welcome Mr M'Cheyne, whose tract on the Lord's Day had been widely circulated and blessed. Many were attracted to hear; interesting congregations assembled in the market-place, and there is reason to believe many were impressed. A person in the town describes Mr M'Cheyne's last address as being peculiarly awakening. He preached in the open air, in a space of ground between the cloth-market and St Nicholas' Church. Above a thousand souls were present, and the service continued till ten, without one person moving from the ground. The moon shone brightly, and the sky was spangled with stars. His subject was "The Great White Throne," (Rev. xx. 11). In concluding his address, he told them, "that they would never meet again till they all met at the Judgment-seat of Christ; but the glorious heavens over their heads, and the bright moon that shone upon them, and the old venerable church behind them, were his witnesses that he had set before them life and death." Some will have cause to remember that night through eternity.[1]

His preaching at Gilsland also was not without effect; and he had good cause to bless the Lord for bringing him through Dumfries-shire on his way homeward. He returned to his people in the beginning of September, full of peace and joy. "I have returned much stronger, indeed quite well. I think I have got some precious souls for my hire on my way home. I earnestly long for more grace and personal holiness, and more usefulness."

The sunsets during that autumn were peculiarly beautiful. Scarcely a day passed but he gazed upon the glowing west after dinner; and as he gazed he would speak of the Sun of Righteousness, or the joy of angels in his presence, or the blessedness of those whose sun can go no more down, till his face shone with gladness as he spoke. And during the winter, he was observed to be peculiarly joyful, being strong in body, and feeling the near presence of Jesus in his soul. He lived

[1] He afterwards preached the same subject with equal impressiveness in the Meadows at Dundee. It was in the open air, and the rain fell heavy, yet the dense crowd stood still to the last.

in the blessed consciousness that he was a child of God, humble and meek, just because he was fully assured that Jehovah was his God and Father. Many often felt that in prayer the name "Holy Father" was breathed with peculiar tenderness and solemnity from his lips.

His flock in St Peter's began to murmur at his absence when again he left them for ten days in November, to assist Mr Hamilton of Regent Square, London, at his communion. But it was his desire for souls that thus led him from place to place, combined with a growing feeling that the Lord was calling him to evangelistic more than to pastoral labours. This visit was a blessed one, and the growth of his soul in holiness was visible to many. During the days of his visit to Mr Hamilton, he read through the Song of Solomon at the time of family worship, commenting briefly on it with rare gracefulness and poetic taste, and yet rarer manifestation of soul-filling love to the Saviour's person. The sanctified affections of his soul, and his insight into the mind of Jesus, seemed to have much affected his friends on these occasions.

Receiving while here an invitation to return by the way of Kelso, he replied :—

LONDON, Nov. 5, 1842.

"MY DEAR HORATIUS,—Our friends here will not let me away till the Friday morning, so that it will require all my diligence to reach Dundee before the Sabbath. I will thus be disappointed of the joy of seeing you, and ministering a word to your dear flock. O that my soul were new moulded, and I were effectually called a second time, and made a vessel full of the Spirit, to tell only of Jesus and his love. I fear I shall never be in this world what I desire. I have preached three times here ; a few tears also have been shed. O for Whitefield's week in London, when a thousand letters came ! The same Jesus reigns ; the same Spirit is able. Why is he restrained ? Is the sin ours ? Are we the bottle-stoppers of these heavenly dews ? Ever yours till glory."

"P.S.—We shall meet, God willing, at the Convocation."

The memorable Convocation met at Edinburgh on November 17th. There were five hundred ministers present from all parts of Scotland. The encroachment of the civil courts upon the prerogatives of Christ, the only Head acknowledged by our Church, and the negligent treatment hitherto given by the legislature of the country to every remonstrance on the part of the Church, had brought on a crisis. The Church of Scotland had maintained from the days of the Reformation that her connection with the State was understood to imply no surrender whatsoever of complete independence in regulating all spiritual matters; and to have allowed any civil authority to control her in doctrine, discipline, or any spiritual act, would have been a daring and flagrant act of treachery to her Lord and King. The deliberations of the Convocation continued during eight days, and the momentous results are well known in this land.

Mr M'Cheyne was never absent from any of the diets of this solemn assembly. He felt the deepest interest in every matter that came before them, got great light as to the path of duty in the course of the consultations, and put his name to all the resolutions, heartily sympathizing in the decided determination that, as a Church of Christ, we must abandon our connection with the State, if our "Claim of Rights" were rejected. These eight days were times of remarkable union and prayerfulness. The proceedings, from time to time, were suspended till the brethren had again asked counsel of the Lord by prayer; and none present will forget the affecting solemnity with which, on one occasion, Mr M'Cheyne poured out our wants before the Lord.

He had a decided abhorrence of Erastianism. When the question was put to him, "Is it our duty to refuse ordination to any one who holds the views of Erastianism?" he replied —"Certainly, whatever be his other qualifications." He was ever a thorough Presbyterian, and used to maintain the necessity of abolishing lay patronage, because, 1. It was not to be found in the Word of God; 2. It destroyed the duty of "trying the spirits;" 3. It meddled with the headship of Christ, coming in between him and his people, saying, "I will place the stars." But still more decided was he in regard to the spiritual independence of the Church. This he reckoned a vital question; and in prospect of the disruption of the

Church of Scotland, if it were denied, he stated at a public meeting—1st, That it was to be deplored in some respects, viz., because of the sufferings of God's faithful servants, the degradation of those who remained behind, the alienation of the aristocracy, the perdition of the ungodly, and the sin of the nation. But, 2nd, It was to be hailed for other reasons—viz., Christ's kingly office would be better known, the truth would be spread into desolate parishes, and faithful ministers would be refined. And when, on March 7th of the following year, the cause of the Church was finally to be pleaded at the bar of the House of Commons, I find him writing—"Eventful night this in the British Parliament! Once more King Jesus stands at an earthly tribunal, and they know him not!"

An interesting anecdote is related of him by a co-presbyter, who returned with him to Dundee after the Convocation. This co-presbyter, Mr Stewart, was conversing with him as to what might be their duty to do in the event of the disruption, and where they might be scattered. Mr Stewart said he could preach in Gaelic, and might go to the Highlanders in Canada, if it were needful. Mr M'Cheyne said—"I think of going to the many thousand convicts that are transported beyond seas, for no man careth for their souls."

We have not many records of his public work after this date. Almost the last note in his diary is dated December 25. "This day ordained four elders, and admitted a fifth, who will all, I trust, be a blessing in this place when I am gone. Was graciously awakened a great while before day, and had two hours alone with God. Preached with much comfort on 1 Tim. v. 17, "Let the elders that rule well," &c. At the end of the sermon and prayer, proposed the regular questions; then made the congregation sing standing; during which time I came down from the pulpit and stood over the four men, then prayed, and all the elders gave the right hand of fellowship, during which I returned to the pulpit, and addressed them and the congregation on their relative duties. Altogether a solemn scene."

The last recorded cases of awakening, and the last entry in his diary, is dated January 6. 1843, "Heard of an awakened soul finding rest—true rest, I trust. Two new cases of awakening; both very deep and touching. At the very time when I was beginning to give up in despair, God gives me tokens of his presence returning."

He here speaks of discouragement, when God for a few months or weeks seemed to be withholding his hand from saving souls. If he was not right in thus hastily forgetting the past for a little, still this feature of his ministry is to be well considered. He entertained so full a persuasion that a faithful minister has every reason to expect to see souls converted under him, that when this was withheld, he began to fear that some hidden evil was provoking the Lord and grieving the Spirit. And ought it not to be so with all of us? Ought we not to suspect, either that we are not living near to God, or that our message is not a true transcript of the glad tidings, in both matter and manner, when we see no souls brought to Jesus? God may certainly hide from our knowledge much of what he accomplishes by our means, but as certainly will he bring to our view some seals of our ministry, in order that our persuasion of being thus sent by him may solemnize and overawe us, as well as lead us on to unwearied labour. Ought it not to be the inscription over the doors of our Assembly and College-halls :—*"Thanks be unto God, which always causeth us to triumph in Christ, and maketh manifest the savour of his knowledge by us in every place;'* 2 Corinthians ii. 14.

About this time, in one of his MSS., there occurs this sentence—"As I was walking in the fields, the thought came over me with almost overwhelming power, that every one of my flock must soon be in heaven or hell. O how I wished that I had a tongue like thunder, that I might make all hear; or that I had a frame like iron, that I might visit every one, and say, 'Escape for thy life!' Ah, sinners! you little know how I fear that you will lay the blame of your damnation at my door."

He was never satisfied with his own attainments in holiness; he was ever ready to learn, and quick to apply, any suggestion that might tend to his greater usefulness. About this period, he used to sing a psalm or hymn every day after dinner. It was often, "The Lord's my Shepherd," &c.; or, "O may we stand before the Lamb," &c. Sometimes it was that hymn, "O for a closer walk with God;" and sometimes the psalm, "O that I like a dove had wings," &c. A friend said of him, "I have sometimes compared him to the silver and graceful ash, with its pensile branches, and leaves of gentle green, reflecting gleams of happy sunshine. The fall of its leaf, too, is like the fall of his—it is green to-night, and gone to-morrow—it does not sere, nor wither."

An experienced servant of God has said, that, while popularity is a snare that few are not caught by, a more subtle and dangerous snare is to be *famed for holiness*. The fame of being a godly man is as great a snare as the fame of being learned or eloquent. It is possible to attend with scrupulous anxiety even to secret habits of devotion, in order to get a name for holiness.[1] If any were exposed to this snare in his day, Mr M'Cheyne was the person. Yet nothing is more certain than that, to the very last, he was ever discovering, and successfully resisting, the deceitful tendencies of his own heart, and a tempting devil. Two things he seems never to have ceased from—the cultivation of personal holiness, and the most anxious efforts to save souls.

About this time he wrote down, for his own use, an examination into things that ought to be amended and changed. I subjoin it entire. How singularly close and impartial are these researches into his soul! How acute is he in discovering his variations from the holy law of God! O that we all were taught by the same spirit thus to try our reins! It is only when we are thus thoroughly experiencing our helplessness, and discovering the thousand forms of indwelling sin, that we really sit as disciples at Christ's feet, and gladly receive him as all in all! And at each such moment we feel in the spirit of Ignatius, *"Νῦν γὰρ ἀρχὴν ἔχω τοῦ μαθητεύεσθαι"* —"It is only now that I begin to be a disciple."

---

[1] How true, yet awful, is the language of Dr Owen (quoted in Bridges' *Christian Ministry,* p. 168). "He that would go down to the pit in peace, let him obtain a great repute for religion; let him preach and labour to make others better than he is himself, and, in the meantime, neglect to humble his heart, to walk with God in manifest holiness and usefulness, and he will not fail of his end."

173

Mr M'Cheyne entitles the examination of his heart and life "*Reformation*," and it commences thus—

"It is the duty of ministers in this day to begin the reformation of religion and manners with themselves, families, &c., with confession of past sin, earnest prayer for direction, grace, and full purpose of heart. Mal. iii. 3. 'He shall purify the sons of Levi.' Ministers are probably laid aside for a time for this very purpose.

"1. *Personal Reformation.*

"I am persuaded that I shall obtain the highest amount of present happiness, I shall do most for God's glory and the good of man, and I shall have the fullest reward in eternity, by maintaining a conscience always washed in Christ's blood, by being filled with the Holy Spirit at all times, and by attaining the most entire likeness to Christ in mind, will, and heart, that it is possible for a redeemed sinner to attain to in this world.

"I am persuaded that whenever any one from without, or my own heart from within, at any moment, or in any circumstances, contradicts this—if any one shall insinuate that it is not for my present and eternal happiness, and for God's glory, and my usefulness, to maintain a blood-washed conscience, to be entirely filled with the Spirit, and to be fully conformed to the image of Christ in all things—that is the voice of the devil, God's enemy, the enemy of my soul, and of all good—the most foolish, wicked, and miserable of all the creatures. See Proverbs ix. 17. 'Stolen waters are sweet.'

"1. *To maintain a conscience void of offence*, I am persuaded that I ought to confess my sins more. I think I ought to confess sin the moment I see it to be sin; whether I am in company, or in study, or even preaching, the soul ought to cast a glance of abhorrence at the sin. If I go on with the duty, leaving the sin unconfessed, I go on with a burdened conscience, and add sin to sin. I think I ought at certain times of the day—my best times—say, after breakfast and after tea—to confess solemnly the sins of the previous hours, and to seek their complete remission.

"I find that the devil often makes use of the confession of sin to stir up again the very sin confessed into new exercise, so that I am afraid to dwell upon the confession. I must ask experienced Christians about this. For the present, I think I should strive against this awful abuse of confession, whereby the devil seeks to frighten me away from confessing. I ought to take all methods for seeing the vileness of my sins. I ought to regard myself as a condemned branch of Adam— as partaker of a nature opposite to God from the womb, Psa. li.—as having a heart full of all wickedness, which pollutes every thought, word, and action, during my whole life, from birth to death. I ought to confess often the sins of my youth, like David and Paul—my sins before conversion, my sins since conversion—sins against light and knowledge—against love and grace—against each person of the Godhead. I ought to look at my sins in the light of the Holy Law—in the light of God's countenance—in the light of the Cross—in the light of the Judgment-seat—in the light of hell—in the light of eternity. I ought to examine my dreams, my floating thoughts —my predilections—my often recurring actions—my habits of thought, feeling, speech, and action—the slanders of my enemies—and the reproofs, and even banterings, of my friends—to find out traces of my prevailing sin—matter for confession. I ought to have a stated day of confession, with fasting—say, once a month. I ought to have a number of scriptures marked, to bring sin to remembrance. I ought to make use of all bodily affliction, domestic trial, frowns of Providence on myself, house, parish, church, or country, as calls from God to confess sin. The sins and afflictions of other men should call me to the same. I ought, on Sabbath evenings, and on Communion Sabbath evenings, to be especially careful to confess the sins of holy things. I ought to confess the sins of my confessions—their imperfections, sinful aims, self-righteous tendency, &c.—and to look to Christ as having confessed my sins perfectly over his own sacrifice.

"I ought to go to Christ for the forgiveness of each sin. In washing my body, I go over every spot, and wash it out: Should I be less careful in washing my soul? I ought to see the stripe that was made on the back of Jesus by each of my sins. I ought to see the infinite pang thrill through the soul of Jesus equal to an eternity of my hell for my sins, and for all of them. I ought to see that in Christ's bloodshedding there is an infinite overpayment for all my sins. Although Christ did not suffer more than infinite justice demanded, yet he could not suffer at all without laying down an infinite ransom.

"I feel, when I have sinned, an immediate reluctance to go to Christ. I am ashamed to go. I feel as if it would do no good to go—as if it were making Christ a minister of sin, to go straight from the swine-trough to the best robe—and a thousand other excuses; but I am persuaded they are all lies, direct from hell. John argues the opposite way—'If any man sin, we have an advocate with the Father;' Jeremiah iii. 1, and a thousand other scriptures are against it. I am sure there is neither peace nor safety from deeper sin, but in going directly to the Lord Jesus Christ. This is God's way of peace and holiness. It is folly to the world and the be-clouded heart, but it is *the way*.

"I must never think a sin too small to need immediate application to the blood of Christ. If I put away a good conscience, concerning faith I make shipwreck. I must never think my sins too great, too aggravated, too presumptuous—as when done on my knees, or in preaching, or by a dying bed, or during dangerous illness—to hinder me from fleeing to Christ. The weight of my sins should act like the weight of a clock, the heavier it is, it makes it go the faster.

"I must not only wash in Christ's blood, but clothe me in Christ's obedience. For every sin of omission in self, I may find a divinely perfect obedience ready for me in Christ. For every sin of commission in self, I may find not only a stripe or a wound in Christ, but also a perfect rendering of the opposite obedience in my place, so that the law is magnified—its curse more than carried—its demand more than answered.

"Often the doctrine of *Christ for me* appears common, well known, having nothing new in it; and I am tempted to pass it by and go to some scripture more taking. This is the devil again—a red-hot lie. *Christ for us* is ever new, ever glorious. 'Unsearchable riches of Christ'—an infinite object, and the only one for a guilty soul. I ought to have a number of Scriptures ready, which lead my blind soul directly to Christ, such as Isaiah xlv., Romans iii.

"2. *To be filled with the Holy Spirit*, I am persuaded that I ought to study more my own weakness. I ought to have a number of scriptures ready to be meditated on, such as Romans vii., John xv., to convince me that I am a helpless worm.

"I am tempted to think that I am now an established Christian—that I have overcome this or that lust so long—that I have got into the habit of the opposite grace—so that there is no fear; I may venture very near the temptation—nearer than other men. This is a lie of Satan. I might as well speak of gunpowder getting by habit a power of resisting fire, so as not to catch the spark. As long as powder is wet it resists the spark; but when it becomes dry it is ready to explode at the first touch. As long as the Spirit dwells in my heart he deadens me to sin, so that, if lawfully called through temptation, I may reckon upon God carrying me through. But when the Spirit leaves me I am like dry gunpowder. O for a sense of this!

"I am tempted to think that there are some sins for which I have no natural taste, such as strong drink, profane language, &c., so that I need not fear temptation to such sins. This is a lie—a proud presumptuous lie. The seeds of all sins are in my heart, and perhaps all the more dangerously that I do not see them.

"I ought to pray and labour for the deepest sense of my utter weakness and helplessness that ever a sinner was brought to feel. I am helpless in respect of every lust that ever was, or ever will be, in the human heart. I am a worm—a beast—before God. I often tremble to think that this is true. I feel as if it would not be safe for me to renounce all indwelling strength, as if it would be dangerous for me to feel (what is the truth) that there is nothing in me keeping me back from the grossest and vilest sin. This is a delusion of the devil. My only safety is to know, feel, and confess my helplessness, that I may hang upon the arm of Omnipotence.

. . . . I daily wish that sin had been rooted out of my heart. I say, 'Why did God leave the roots of lasciviousness, pride, anger, &c., in my bosom. He hates sin, and I hate it; why did he not take it clean away?' I know many answers to this which completely satisfy my judgment, but still I do not *feel* satisfied. This is wrong. It is right to be weary of the being of sin, but not right to quarrel with my present 'good fight of faith.' . . . . . The falls of professors into sin make me tremble. I have been driven away from prayer, and burdened in a fearful manner by hearing or seeing their sin. This is wrong. It is right to tremble, and to make every sin of every professor a lesson of my own helplessness, but it should lead me the more to Christ. . . . If I were more deeply convinced of my utter helplessness, I think I would not be so alarmed when I hear of the falls of other men. . . . . I should study those sins in which I am most helpless, in which passion becomes like a whirlwind and I like a straw. No figure of speech can represent my utter want of power to resist the torrent of sin. . . . I ought to study Christ's omnipotence more; Heb. vii. 25; I Thess. v. 23; Rom. vi. 14; Rom. v. 9, 10; and such scriptures should be ever before me. . . . . Paul's thorn, 2 Cor. xii., is the experience of the greater part of my life. It should be ever before me. . . . . There are many subsidiary methods of seeking deliverance from sins, which must not be neglected—thus, marriage, 1 Cor. vii. 2; fleeing, 1 Tim. vi. 11, 1 Cor. vi. 18; watch and pray, Matt. xxvi. 41; the Word, 'It is written, It is written.' So Christ defended himself; Matt. iv. . . . . But the main defence is casting myself into the arms of Christ like a helpless child, and beseeching him to fill me with the Holy Spirit; 'This is the victory that overcometh the world, even our faith,' 1 John v. 4, 5— a wonderful passage.

"I ought to study Christ as a living Saviour more—as a Shepherd, carrying the sheep he finds—as a King, reigning in and over the souls he has redeemed—as a Captain, fighting with those who fight with me, Ps. xxxv.—as one who has engaged to bring me through all temptations and trials, however impossible to flesh and blood.

"I am often tempted to say, How can this man save us?

How can Christ in heaven deliver me from lusts which I feel raging in me, and nets I feel enclosing me? This is the father of lies again! 'He is able to save unto the uttermost.'

"I ought to study Christ as an Intercessor. He prayed most for Peter who was to be most tempted. I am on his breastplate. If I could hear Christ praying for me in the next room, I would not fear a million of enemies. Yet the distance makes no difference; he is praying for me.

"I ought to study the Comforter more—his Godhead, his love, his almightiness. I have found by experience that nothing sanctifies me so much as meditating on the Comforter, as John xiv. 16. And yet how seldom I do this! Satan keeps me from it. I am often like those men who said, They knew not if there be any Holy Ghost. . . . . . I ought never to forget that my body is dwelt in by the Third Person of the Godhead. The very thought of this should make me tremble to sin, 1 Cor. vi. . . . . I ought never to forget that sin grieves the Holy Spirit—vexes and quenches him. . . . . . If I would be filled with the Spirit, I feel I must read the Bible more, pray more, and watch more.

"3. *To gain entire likeness to Christ*, I ought to get a high esteem of the happiness of it. I am persuaded that God's happiness is inseparably linked in with his holiness. Holiness and happiness are like light and heat. God never tasted one of the pleasures of sin.

"Christ had a body such as I have, yet he never tasted one of the pleasures of sin. The redeemed, through all eternity, will never taste one of the pleasures of sin; yet their happiness is complete. It would be my greatest happiness to be from this moment entirely like them. Every sin is something away from my greatest enjoyment. . . . The devil strives night and day to make me forget this or disbelieve it. He says, Why should you not enjoy this pleasure as much as Solomon or David? You may go to heaven also. I am persuaded that this is a lie—that my true happiness is to go and sin no more.

"I ought not to delay parting with sins. Now is God's time. 'I made haste and delayed not.' . . . I ought not to spare sins, because I have long allowed them as infirmities; and others would think it odd if I were to change all at once. What a wretched delusion of Satan that is!

"Whatever I see to be sin, I ought from this hour to set my whole soul against it, using all scriptural methods to mortify it—as, the Scriptures, special prayer for the Spirit, fasting, watching.

"I ought to mark strictly the occasions when I have fallen, and avoid the occasion as much as the sin itself.

"Satan often tempts me to go as near to temptations as possible, without committing the sin. This is fearful—tempting God and grieving the Holy Ghost. It is a deep-laid plot of Satan.

"I ought to flee all temptation, according to Prov. iv. 15 —'Avoid it, pass not by it, turn from it, and pass away.' . . . . . I ought constantly to pour out my heart to God, praying for entire conformity to Christ—for the whole law to be written on my heart. . . . . I ought statedly and solemnly to give my heart to God—to surrender my all into his everlasting arms, according to the prayer—Ps. xxxi., 'Into thine hand I commit my spirit'—beseeching him not to let any iniquity, secret or presumptuous, have dominion over me, and to fill me with every grace that is in Christ in the highest degree that it is possible for a redeemed sinner to receive it, and at all times, till death.

"I ought to meditate often on heaven as a world of holiness—where all are holy, where the joy is holy joy, the work holy work; so that, without personal holiness, I never can be there. . . . . I ought to avoid the appearance of evil. God commands me; and I find that Satan has a singular art in linking the appearance and reality together.

"I find that speaking of some sins defiles my mind and leads me into temptation; and I find that God forbids even saints to speak of the things that are done of them in secret. I ought to avoid this.

"Eve, Achan, David, all fell through the lust of the eye. I should make a covenant with mine, and pray, 'Turn away mine eyes from viewing vanity.' . . . . . Satan makes unconverted men like the deaf adder to the sound of the gospel. I should pray to be made deaf by the Holy Spirit to all that would tempt me to sin.

"One of my most frequent occasions of being led into temptation is this—I say it is needful to my office that I listen to this, or look into this, or speak of this. So far this is true; yet I am sure Satan has his part in this argument. I should seek divine direction to settle how far it will be good for my ministry, and how far evil for my soul, that I may avoid the latter.

"I am persuaded that nothing is thriving in my soul unless it is growing. 'Grow in grace.' 'Lord, increase our faith.' 'Forgetting the things that are behind.' . . . . . . I am persuaded that I ought to be enquiring at God and man what grace I want, and how I may become more like Christ. . . . . . . I ought to strive for more purity, humility, meekness, patience under suffering, love. 'Make me Christ-like in all things,' should be my constant prayer. 'Fill me with the Holy Spirit.'

"2. *Reformation in Secret Prayer.*

"I ought not to omit any of the parts of prayer—confession, adoration, thanksgiving, petition, and intercession.

"There is a fearful tendency to omit *confession*, proceeding from low views of God and his law—slight views of my heart and the sins of my past life. This must be resisted. There is a constant tendency to omit *adoration*, when I forget to whom I am speaking—when I rush heedlessly into the presence of Jehovah, without remembering his awful name and character—when I have little eyesight for his glory, and little admiration of his wonders. 'Where are the wise?' I have the native tendency of the heart to omit *giving thanks*. And yet it is specially commanded, Phil. iv. 6. Often when the heart is selfish—dead to the salvation of others—I omit *intercession*. And yet it especially is the spirit of the Great Advocate, who has the name of Israel always on his heart.

"Perhaps every prayer need not have all these; but surely a day should not pass without some space being devoted to each.

"I ought to pray before seeing any one. Often when I sleep long, or meet with others early, and then have family prayer, and breakfast, and forenoon callers, often it is eleven or twelve o'clock before I begin secret prayer. This is a wretched system. It is unscriptural. Christ rose before day, and went into a solitary place. David says, 'Early will I seek thee; thou shalt early hear my voice.' Mary Magdalene came to the sepulchre while it was yet dark. Family prayer loses much of its power and sweetness; and I can do no good to those who come to seek from me. The conscience feels guilty, the soul unfed, the lamp not trimmed. Then, when secret prayer comes, the soul is often out of tune. I feel it is far better to begin with God—to see his face first—to get my soul near him before it is near another. 'When I awake I am still with thee.'

"If I have slept too long, or am going an early journey, or my time is any way shortened, it is best to dress hurriedly, and have a few minutes alone with God, than to give it up for lost.

"But, in general, it is best to have at least one hour *alone with God*, before engaging in anything else. At the same time, I must be careful not to reckon communion with God by minutes or hours, or by solitude. I have pored over my Bible, and on my knees for hours, with little or no communion; and my times of solitude have been often times of greatest temptation.

"As to *intercession*, I ought daily to intercede for my own family, connections, relatives, and friends; also for my flock —the believers, the awakened, the careless; the sick, the bereaved; the poor, the rich; my elders, Sabbath-school teachers, day-school teachers, children, tract-distributors— that all means may be blessed. Sabbath-day preaching and teaching; visiting of the sick, visiting from house to house; providences, sacraments. I ought daily to intercede briefly for the whole town, the Church of Scotland, all faithful ministers; for vacant congregations, students of divinity, &c.; for dear brethren by name; missionaries to Jews and Gentiles; and for this end I must read missionary intelligence regularly, and get acquainted with all that is doing throughout the world. It would stir me up to pray with the map before me. I must have a scheme of prayer, also the names of missionaries marked on the map. I ought to intercede at large for the above on Saturday morning and evening from seven to eight. Perhaps also I might take different parts for different days; only I ought daily to plead for my family and flock. I ought to pray in everything. 'Be careful for nothing, but in *everything* . . . . . by prayer and supplication, make your requests known unto God." Often I receive a letter asking to preach, or some such request. I find myself answering before having asked counsel of God. Still oftener a person calls and asks me something, and I do not ask direction. Often I go out to visit a sick person in a hurry, without asking His blessing, which alone can make the visit of any use. I am persuaded that I ought never to do anything without prayer, and, if possible, special, secret prayer.

"In reading the history of the Church of Scotland, I see how much her troubles and trials have been connected with the salvation of souls and the glory of Christ. I ought to pray far more for our Church, for our leading ministers by name, and for my own clear guidance in the right way, that I may not be led aside, or driven aside, from following Christ. Many difficult questions may be forced on us for which I am not fully prepared, such as the lawfulness of Covenants. I should pray much more in peaceful days, that I may be guided rightly when days of trial come.

"I ought to spend the best hours of the day in communion with God. It is my noblest and most fruitful employment, and is not to be thrust into any corner. The morning hours, from six to eight, are the most uninterrupted, and should be thus employed, if I can prevent drowsiness. A little time after breakfast might be given to intercession. After tea is my best hour, and that should be solemnly dedicated to God, if possible.

"I ought not to give up the good old habit of prayer before going to bed; but guard must be kept against sleep; planning what things I am to ask is the best remedy. When I awake in the night, I ought to rise and pray, as David and as John Welsh did.

"I ought to read three chapters of the Bible in secret every day, at least.

"I ought on Sabbath morning to look over all the chapters read through the week, and especially the verses marked. I ought to read in three different places; I ought also to read according to subjects, lives," &c.

He has evidently left this unfinished, and now he knows even as he is known.

Toward the end of his ministry, he became peculiarly jealous of becoming an idol to his people; for he was loved and revered by many who gave no evidence of love to Christ. This often pained him much. It is indeed right in a people to regard their pastor with no common love, 2 Cor. ix. 14, but there is ever a danger ready to arise. He used to say, "Ministers are but the pole; it is to the brazen serpent you are to look."

The state of his health would not permit him to be laborious in going from house to house, whereas preaching and evangelistic work in general was less exhausting; but of course, while he was thus engaged, many concerns of the parish would be unattended to, accordingly his Session offered him a stated assistant to help him in his parochial duty. With this proposal he at once concurred. Mr Gatherer, then at Caraldstone, was chosen, and continued to labour faithfully with him during the remaining days of his ministry.

In the beginning of the year he published his *"Daily Bread,"* an arrangement of Scripture, that the Bible might be read through in the course of a year. He sought to induce his people to meditate much on the written Word in all its breadth. His last publication was *"Another Lily Gathered,"* or the account of James Laing, a little boy in his flock, brought to Christ early, and carried soon to glory.

In the middle of January 1843, he visited Collace, and preached on 1 Cor. ix. 27, "A Castaway"—a sermon so solemn that one said it was like a blast of the trumpet that would awaken the dead. Next day he rode on to Lintrathen, where the people were willing to give up their work at mid-day, if he would come and preach to them. All this month he was breathing after glory. In his letters there are such expressions as these: "I often pray, Lord, make me as holy as a pardoned sinner can be made." "Often, often I would like to depart and be with Christ—to mount to Pisgah-top and take a farewell look of the Church below, and leave my body and be present with the Lord. Ah, it is far better!" Again: "I do not expect to live long. I expect a sudden call some day—perhaps soon—and therefore I speak very plainly." But, indeed, he had long been persuaded that his course would be brief. His hearers remember well how often he would speak in such language as that with which he one day closed his sermon. "Changes are coming; every eye before me shall soon be dim in death. Another pastor shall feed this flock; another singer lead the psalm; another flock shall fill this fold."

In the beginning of February, by appointment of the Committee of the Convocation, he accompanied Mr Alexander of Kirkcaldy to visit the districts of Deer and Ellon—districts over which he yearned, for Moderatism had held undisputed sway over them for generations. It was to be his last evangelistic tour. He exemplified his own remark, "The oil of the lamp in the temple burnt away in giving light; so should we."

He set out, says one that saw him leave town, as unclouded and happy as the sky that was above his head that bright morning. During the space of three weeks, he preached or spoke at meetings in four-and-twenty places, sometimes more than once in the same place. Great impression was made upon the people of the district. One who tracked his footsteps a month after his death states that sympathy with the principles of our suffering Church was awakened in many places; but above all, a thirst was excited for the pure Word of Life. His eminently holy walk and conversation, combined with the deep solemnity of his preaching, was specially felt. The people loved to speak of him. In one place, where a meeting had been intimated, the people assembled, resolving to cast stones at him as soon as he should begin to speak; but no sooner had he begun, than his manner, his look, his words, riveted them all, and they listened with intense earnestness; and before he left the place, the people gathered round him, entreating him to stay and preach to them. One man, who had cast mud at him, was afterwards moved to tears on hearing of his death.

He wrote to Mr Gatherer, February 14th, "I had a nice opportunity of preaching in Aberdeen; and in Peterhead our meeting was truly successful. The minister of St Fergus I found to be what you described. We had a solemn meeting in his Church. In Strichen, we had a meeting in the Independent Meeting-house. On Friday evening, we had two delightful meetings, in a mill at Crechie, and in the church of Clola. The people were evidently much impressed, some weeping. On Saturday evening we met in the Brucklay barn. I preached on Sabbath, at New Deer in the morning, and at Fraserburgh in the evening—both interesting meetings. To-night we meet in Pitsligo church. To-morrow we trust to be in Aberdour; and then we leave for the Presbytery of Ellon. The weather has been delightful till now. To-day, the snow is beginning to drift. But God is with us, and he will carry us to the very end. I am quite well, though a little fatigued sometimes." On the 24th, he writes to another friend, "To-day is the first we have rested since leaving home, so that I am almost overcome with fatigue. Do not be idle; improve in all useful knowledge. You know what an enemy I am to idleness."

Never was it more felt that God was with him than in this journey. The Lord seemed to show in him the meaning of the text, "Out of his belly shall flow rivers of living water." John vii. 38. Even when silent, the near intercourse he held with God left its impression on those around. His *constant holiness* touched the conscience of many.

Returning to his beloved flock on March 1st, in good health, but much exhausted, he related next evening, at his prayer-meeting, what things he had seen and heard. During the next twelve days, he was to be found going out and in among his people, filling up, as his manner was, every inch of time. But he had been much weakened by his unceasing exertions when in the north, and so was more than ordinarily exposed to the typhus fever that was then prevailing in his parish, several cases of which he visited in his enfeebled state.

On Sabbath the 5th, he preached three times; and two days after, I find him writing to his father: "All domestic matters go on like a placid stream—I trust not without its fertilizing influence. Nothing is more improving than the domestic altar, when we come to it for a daily supply of soul nourishment." To the last we get glances into his soul's growth. His family devotions were full of life and full of gladness to the end. Indeed, his very manner in reading the chapter reminded you of a man boring into the sands for pieces of fine gold, and from time to time holding up to you what he delighted to have found.

On Sabbath the 12th, he preached upon Heb. ix. 15, in the forenoon, and Rom. ix. 22, 23, in the afternoon, with uncommon solemnity; and it was observed, both then and on other late occasions, he spoke with peculiar strength upon the sovereignty of God. These were his last discourses to his people in St Peter's. That same evening, he went down to Broughty Ferry, and preached upon Isaiah lx. 1, "Arise, shine," &c. It was the last time he was to be engaged directly in proclaiming Christ to sinners; and as he began his ministry with souls for his hire, so it appears that his last discourse had in it saving power to some, and that rather from the holiness it breathed than from the wisdom of its words. After his death, a note was found unopened, which had been sent to him in the course of the following week, when he lay in the fever. It ran thus: "I hope you will pardon a stranger for addressing to you a few lines. I heard you preach last Sabbath evening, and it pleased God to bless that sermon to my soul. It was not so much what you said, as your manner of speaking, that struck me. I saw in you a beauty in holiness that I never saw before. You also said something in your prayer that struck me very much. It was, *'Thou knowest that we love thee.'* O Sir, what would I give that I could say to my blessed Saviour, 'Thou knowest that I love thee.'"

Next evening he held a meeting in St Peter's, with the view of organizing his people for collecting in behalf of the Free Protesting Church—the disruption of the Establishment being now inevitable. He spoke very fervently; and after the meeting felt chilled and unwell. Next morning he felt that he was ill, but went out in the afternoon to the marriage of two of his flock. He seemed, however, to anticipate a serious attack, for, on his way home, he made some arrangements connected with his ministerial work, and left a message at Dr Gibson's house, asking him to come and see him. He believed that he had taken the fever, and it was so. That night he lay down upon the bed from which he was never to rise. He spoke little; but intimated that he apprehended danger.

On Wednesday, he said he thought that he would never have seen the morning, he felt so sore broken, and had got no sleep; but afterwards added, "Shall we receive good at the hand of the Lord, and shall we not receive evil also?" He seemed clouded in spirit, often repeating such passages as— "My moisture is turned into the drought of summer;" "My bones wax old, through my roaring all day long." It was with difficulty that he was able to speak a few words with his assistant, Mr Gatherer. In the forenoon, Mr Miller of Wallacetown found him oppressed with extreme pain in his head. Amongst other things they conversed upon Psalm cxxvi. On coming to the 6th verse, Mr M'Cheyne said he would give him a division of it. 1. *What is sowed*—"Precious seed." 2. *The manner of sowing it*—"Goeth forth and weepeth." He dwelt upon *"weepeth,"* and then said, "Ministers should go forth at all times." 3. *The fruit*—"Shall doubtless come again with rejoicing." Mr Miller pointed to the *certainty* of it; Mr M'Cheyne assented, "Yes—*doubtless.*" After praying with him, Mr Miller repeated Matthew xi. 28, upon which Mr M'Cheyne clasped his hands with great earnestness. As he became worse his medical attendants forbade him to be visited. Once or twice he asked for me, and was heard to speak of *"Smyrna,"* as if the associations of his illness there were recalled by his burning fever now. I was not at that time aware of his danger, even the rumour of it had not reached us.

Next day, he continued sunk in body and mind, till about the time when his people met for their usual evening prayer-meeting, when he requested to be left alone for half an hour. When his servant entered the room again, he exclaimed with a joyful voice, "My soul is escaped, as a bird out of the snare of the fowler; the snare is broken, and I am escaped." His countenance, as he said this, bespoke inward peace. Ever after he was observed to be happy; and at supper-time that evening, when taking a little refreshment, he gave thanks, "For strength in the time of weakness—for light in the time of darkness—for joy in the time of sorrow—for comforting us in all our tribulations, that we may be able to comfort those that are in any trouble, by the comfort wherewith we ourselves are comforted of God."

On Sabbath, when one expressed a wish that he had been able to go forth as usual to preach, he replied, "My thoughts are not your thoughts, neither are my ways your ways, saith the Lord;" and added, "I am preaching the sermon that God would have me to do."

On Tuesday (the 21st) his sister read to him several hymns. The last words he heard, and the last he seemed to understand, were those of Cowper's hymn, "Sometimes a light surprises the Christian as he sings." And then the delirium came on.

At one time, during the delirium, he said to his attendant, "Mind the text, 1 Corinth. xv. 58. Be steadfast, unmoveable, always abounding in the work of the Lord," dwelling with much emphasis on the last clause, *"forasmuch as ye know that your labour is not in vain in the Lord."* At another time, he seemed to feel himself among his brethren, and said, "I don't think much of policy in church courts; no, I hate it; but I'll tell you what I like, faithfulness to God, and a holy walk." His voice, which had been weak before, became very strong now; and often was he heard speaking to or praying for his people. "You must be awakened in time, or you will be awakened in everlasting torment, to your eternal confusion!" "You may soon get me away, but that will not save your souls!" Then he prayed, "This parish, Lord, this people, this whole place!" At another time, "Do it thyself, Lord, for thy weak servant!" And again, as if praying for the saints,

189

"Holy Father, keep through thine own name those whom thou hast given me!"

Thus he continued most generally engaged, while the delirium lasted, either in prayer or in preaching to his people, and always apparently in happy frame, till the morning of Saturday the 25th. On that morning, while his kind medical attendant, Dr Gibson, stood by, he lifted up his hands as if in the attitude of pronouncing the blessing, and then sank down. Not a groan or a sigh, but only a quiver of the lip, and his soul was at rest.

As he was subject to frequent sickness, it was not till within some days of his death that serious alarm was generally felt, and hence the stroke came with awful suddenness upon us all. That same afternoon, while preparing for Sabbath duties, the tidings reached me. I hastened down, though scarce knowing why I went. His people were that evening met together in the church, and such a scene of sorrow has not often been witnessed in Scotland. It was like the weeping for King Josiah. Hundreds were there; the lower part of the church was full : and none among them seemed able to contain their sorrow. Every heart seemed bursting with grief, so that the weeping and the cries could be heard afar off. The Lord had most severely wounded the people whom he had before so peculiarly favoured; and now, by this awful stroke of his hand, was fixing deeper in their souls all that his servant had spoken in the days of his peculiar ministry.

Wherever the news of his departure came, every Christian countenance was darkened with sadness. Perhaps, never was the death of one, whose sole occupation had been preaching the everlasting gospel, more felt by all the saints of God in Scotland. Not a few also of our Presbyterian brethren in Ireland felt the blow to the very heart. He used himself to say, "Live so as to be missed;" and none that saw the tears that were shed over his death would have doubted that his own life had been what he recommended to others. He had not completed more than twenty-nine years when God took him.

On the day of his burial, business was quite suspended in the parish. The streets, and every window, from the house to the grave, were crowded with those who felt that a Prince in Israel had fallen; and many a careless man felt a secret awe creep over his hardened soul as he cast his eye on the solemn spectacle.

His tomb may be seen on the pathway at the north-west corner of St Peter's burying-ground. He has gone to the "mountain of myrrh and the hill of frankincense, till the day break and the shadows flee away." His work was finished! His heavenly Father had not another plant for him to water, nor another vine for him to train; and the Saviour who so loved him was waiting to greet him with his own welcome—"Well done, good and faithful servant, enter thou into the joy of thy Lord."

But what is the voice to us? Has this been sent as the stroke of wrath, or the rebuke of love? "His way is in the sea, and his path in the great waters, and his footsteps are not known." Only this much we can clearly see, that nothing was more fitted to leave his character and example impressed on our remembrance for ever than his early death. There might be envy while he lived; there is none now. There might have been some of the youthful attractiveness of his graces lost had he lived many years; this cannot be impaired now. It seems as if the Lord had struck the flower from its stem, ere any of the colours had lost their bright hue, or any leaf its fragrance.

Well may the flock of St Peter's lay it to heart. They have had days of visitation. Ye have seen the right hand of the Lord plucked out of his bosom! What shall the unsaved among you do in the day of the Lord's anger! "If thou hadst known, even thou, at least in this thy day, the things which belong to thy peace!"

It has been more than once the lot of Scotland (as was said in the days of Durham) to enjoy so much of the Lord's kindness, as to have men to lose whose loss has been felt to the very heart—witnesses for Christ, who saw the King's face and testified of his beauty. We cannot weep them back; but shall we not call upon Him with whom is the residue of the Spirit, that ere the Lord come, he would raise up men, like Enoch or like Paul, who shall reach nearer the stature of the perfect man, and bear witness with more power to all nations? Are there not (as he who has left us used to hope) "better ministers in store for Scotland than any that have yet arisen!"

Ministers of Christ, does not the Lord call upon us especially? Many of us are like the angel of the Church of Ephesus: we have "works, and labour, and patience, and cannot bear them that are evil, and we have borne, and for his name's sake we labour, and have not fainted;" but we want the fervour of "first love." O how seldom now do we hear of fresh supplies of holiness arriving from the heavenly places (Eph. i. 3)—new grace appearing among the saints, and in living ministers! We get contented with our old measure and kind, as if the windows of heaven were never to be opened. Few among us see the lower depths of the horrible pit; few ever enter the inner chambers of the house of David.

But there has been one among us who, ere he had reached the age at which a priest in Israel would have been entering on his course, dwelt at the Mercy-seat as if it were his home —preached the certainties of eternal life with an undoubting mind—and spent his nights and days in ceaseless breathings after holiness, and the salvation of sinners. Hundreds of souls were his reward from the Lord, ere he left us; and in him have we been taught how much one man may do who will only press farther into the presence of his God, and handle more skilfully the unsearchable riches of Christ, and speak more boldly for his God. We speak much against unfaithful ministers, while we ourselves are awfully unfaithful! Are we never afraid that the cries of souls whom we have betrayed to perdition through our want of personal holiness, and our defective preaching of Christ crucified, may ring in our ears for ever? Our Lord is at the door. In the twinkling of an eye our work will be done. "Awake, awake, O arm of the Lord, awake as in the ancient days," till every one of thy pastors be willing to impart to the flock, over which the Holy Ghost has made him overseer, not the Gospel of God only, but also his own soul. And O that each one were able, as he stands in the pastures feeding thy sheep and lambs, to look up and appeal to thee—*"Lord, thou knowest all things! thou knowest that I love thee!"*